TOWN

D1473348

Toy Horse No. 171 1982
Collage, gouache, mechanical pen and ink,
steel pen, reversed

TOWN

D A V I D B U R N E T T

ART GALLERY OF ONTARIO / McCLELLAND AND STEWART LIMITED TORONTO

CANADIAN CATALOGUING IN
PUBLICATION DATA

Burnett, David.
Town

Bibliography
ISBN 0-7710-1781-2

1. Town, Harold, 1924-   — Exhibitions.
I. Town, Harold, 1924-   II. Art Gallery
of Ontario.   III. Title.

ND249.T69A4 1986   759.11   C86-093128-5

Financial support from the Canada Council
for the publication of the book is gratefully
acknowledged.

On the Cover:
In Memory of Emelio del Junco 1974-75
Oil and lucite on canvas, detail

CONTENTS

LENDERS TO THE EXHIBITION

A.G.F. Management Limited

Art Gallery of Hamilton

Art Gallery of Ontario

Art Gallery of Windsor

Mr. & Mrs. P. Berton

Mrs. Dorothy Cameron-Bloore

Canada Council Art Bank

Mr. H. Spencer Clark

Mr. Garth H. Drabinsky

Fred G. Garner

Joan and Martin Goldfarb

The Solomon R. Guggenheim Museum

Mr. & Mrs. R. Campbell-Hain

Mr. & Mrs. W.B. Herman

The Imperial Life Assurance Company of Canada

Mr. & Mrs. H. Klamer

Mr. James G. Laidlaw

Dr. and Mrs. G. Lautenschlaeger

London Regional Art Gallery

Mackenzie Art Gallery

The Metropolitan Museum of Art

The Montreal Museum of Fine Arts

The Museum of Modern Art

National Gallery of Canada

Karen and Raymond Oster

Mr. and Mrs. Nicholas Rallis

Sam and Esther Sarick

Sarnia Public Library and Art Gallery

Mr. and Mrs. J. Shadbolt

Gloria Shulman

Mr. & Mrs. L. Trevor

University of Lethbridge Art Gallery

Vancouver Art Gallery

Mrs. O.D. Vaughan

Dr. and Mrs. Sydney L. Wax

Jessica and Percy Waxer

and private collections

Muscleman 1983
Oil and lucite on canvas

Musclemen 1983
Oil and lucite on canvas

PREFACE

Harold Town has been one of the most forceful personalities on the Canadian art scene for nearly forty years. He first showed at the Art Gallery of Toronto, as it was called then, in 1946, when one of his paintings was selected by the jury for inclusion in the 74th Annual Exhibition of the Ontario Society of Artists. Now he is welcomed at the Art Gallery of Ontario with a retrospective comprising more than two hundred and thirty works.

Characteristic of Harold Town's work has been the range and fertility of his creative imagination and his ability to transform this, by painting, drawing, collage and printmaking, into continual pictorial surprise. Characteristic too is his commitment to his work. This exhibition can, therefore, be a retrospective only for the time being. More than a quarter of the works included have never been exhibited before, and with the recent collages, the *Muscleman* paintings and *The Famous* drawings, we are seeing, for the first time, series of work that are still in active development. It is inevitable that with such a rich range to look at, and so many memories, each of us will find particular areas of his work that have special meaning or give particular pleasure to us. The value of an exhibition such as this is that we have the opportunity to both review our understanding and broaden the range of our appreciation.

This exhibition was initiated by Dr. David Burnett when he was Curator of Contemporary Canadian Art at the Art Gallery of Ontario. After he left the Gallery in November 1984 he continued to work, as a guest curator, on the production of the exhibition. He has also written this book that accompanies the exhibition. We are delighted that, once again, McClelland and Stewart has joined with us to co-publish a book celebrating a major exhibition of one of Canada's well-known artists.

It is with special pleasure that the Art Gallery of Ontario invites you to join with us in honouring an artist who has contributed so strongly to the character of art in Canada.

William J. Withrow
Director
Art Gallery of Ontario

Lillian Gish 1926 1984
Pencil on acid-free matt board

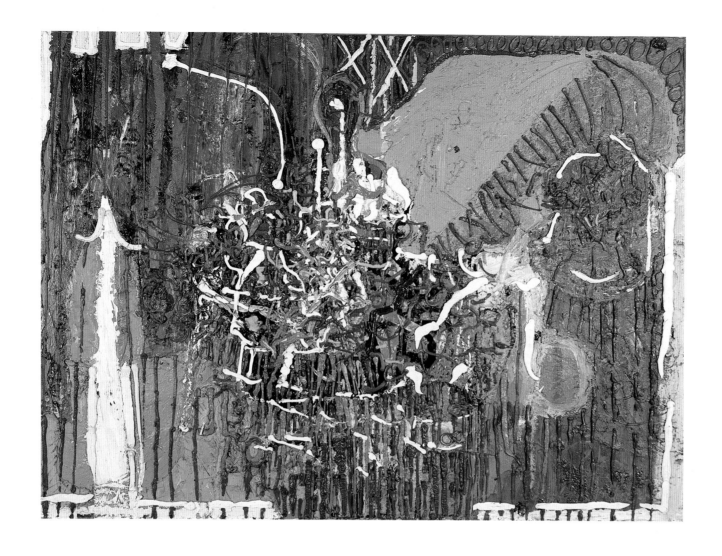

The Turner Reprise 1958-60
Oil and lucite on masonite

Music Behind 1958-59
Collage

FOREWORD

A character in a Mavis Gallant short story believed that "God hates art, the trifling rival creation." God has nothing to fear; all art is imperfect and sometimes, as in the case of Cézanne, is at its greatest when marinated in failure and served up on the spoon of impossible aspiration. Unfortunately, most of the judgements surrounding any work of art have very little to do with the matrix of content, or the stretching line of intention. To a great extent this is as it should be.... for if art could be absolutely verified as to importance in, say, the way gold can be judged for purity and weight, then it would of course be finished as a mythic activity. Free of doubt, controversy, and the inexplicable fluctuation of reputation, art-making would bear the same relationship to creativity as cake mix does to baking.

A retrospective or survey exhibition reverses the Dorian Gray process. The artist discovers the painting of his youth and hopes to find a reflecting surface in the full bloom of spring that bounces the eye about and rings like a bell. Retrospectives are funerals at which the corpse, your youth, is expected to give a sparkling eulogy to the present. However, for the art worker there is no real past, no actual present; the present is always the next idea, the next stroke...the nexus of the next...even though you may regret the omissions, the lost and absent works that in memory appeared under your hand in one jump, as suddenly as a sneeze. It is tomorrow that counts.

Then you remind yourself that you paint because you have to, which is hardly praiseworthy or deserving of note, and that the greatest reward, indeed possibly the only one, excepting that your life has been free of boredom, comes when you discover something done long ago, of which you have no memory, and realize that it works, still pops and glows and has some fraction of the unobtainable perfection that we all strive for.

Along the way there have been many people who have helped me and stood by the work from the beginning: the late Pearl McCarthy and notably Robert Fulford, who always seemed to be there...not as a power broker or proselytizer, but with Shavian clarity of style, simply there.

I owe much to the Director Emeritus of the Art Gallery of Windsor, Kenneth Saltmarche who, despite the fact that as an art student I helped hoist him onto the top of a piano while he was stuffed in a waste paper basket, has been acerbically supportive, along with his curator, Ted Fraser, who never raises a damp finger to the wind. My thanks, too, to Jack McClelland, who has, through a distinguished career that stretches from goalie to publisher, lost neither his nerve, verve or sense of honour; and to Gary Dault, the grizzled conscience of Canadian Art Criticism, who touched me with his absolute loathing of some of my painting.

Finally I have to thank David and Marilyn Burnett, whose felicitous partnership, concern for historical accuracy, and exponential belief in the work made the exhibition possible; and lastly, for saying yes and giving me the surprise of my life, William Withrow, Director of the Art Gallery of Ontario.

Harold Town

Harold Town has been, for more than forty years, a prolific, complex, and demanding artist. His *oeuvre* comprises many thousands of pieces in a wide range of media. The complexity of the work lies not only in its range over time, but also in its contrasting approaches at each particular moment. A retrospective of Town's work cannot, therefore, simply chart a developmental course, but must seek to reflect through its changes and constants, its internal contrasts and external responses, and its innovations and criticisms, the integrity of his artistic production. I decided, in selecting the exhibition, to concentrate on particular series of works, making a broad selection from each series, rather than to include representative examples of every series that he has made.

Working within those parameters, the organization of the exhibition and production of this book has been a complex operation involving many people. My thanks go first to Harold Town, who has given me so much of his time, and who has tirelessly searched his records, his storage, and his memory. I could not begin to estimate how many works we have looked at together – the final selections amount to only a tiny fraction of his extraordinary production – but I will remember the pleasure of seeing so much with him, his wit both spoken and painted, and his complete professionalism in the relationship between curator and artist.

The two other people who have been central to this enterprise are my wife Marilyn and Charis Wahl. In all the arrangements for the exhibition and the book, the work has been a joint effort between Marilyn and myself; her work has been integral to every aspect. Neither the book nor the exhibition could have come about without her. Charis Wahl has not only edited my text, but has coordinated the production of the book among McClelland and Stewart, the Art Gallery of Ontario, and myself. I am grateful to her for the clarity and sensibility she brought to editing the text, and for her sound skills in guiding the project through to completion.

My special thanks go to Jack McClelland, Jan Walter, and Jan Coughtrey at McClelland and Stewart; to Helene and Brent Mazelow at the Mazelow Gallery; to Ron Moore at the Moore Gallery; and, at the Art Gallery of Ontario, to Philip Monk, Curator of Contemporary Canadian Art, to Cheryl Izen and Mara Meikle; to Maia-Mari Sutnik, Coordinator, Photographic Services and her assistant Faye Van Horne; to Ivan Holmes, Designer, and Catherine Van Baren, Editor.

Finally I am most grateful to all those people who have generously lent works in their possession to this exhibition. My requests have invariably been met with warmth and enthusiasm, and although I cannot list each person here, my appreciation is still expressed individually.

David Burnett

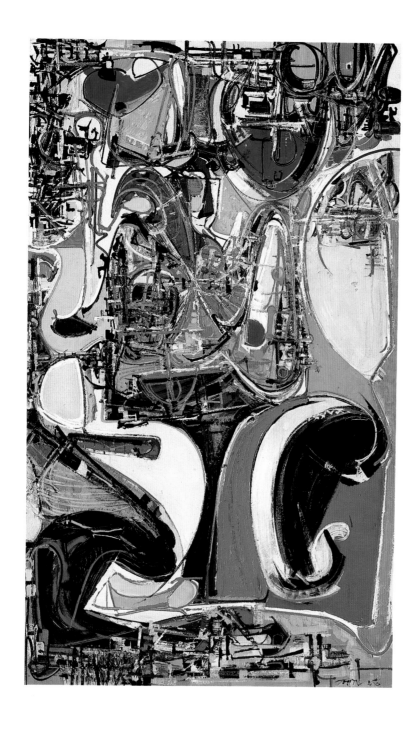

Through Forest the Jungle of Industry c. 1954
Oil on masonite

Entrance of the Stage Left Dragon 1960
Collage

INTRODUCTION

For some people biography must be preceded by autobiography. Harold Town is such a person. There is nothing anyone could reconstruct from interviews and documentation that would come close to the tone and wit and texture of detail with which he would fill a book he wrote himself.

Yet the essential and objective point of transformation exists in his work, in the paintings and drawings, prints and collages he has made for more than forty years. Their character is infused with that tone and wit and texture, just as their surfaces are formed by a touch as sure and unique as a fingerprint. In his rigorous pursuit of independence, the relationship of art and expression in the work is completely personal. Equally, however, it insists that whatever has been of value in the art of other times and other places bears, both as a credit and a responsibility, on the art made in this place and at this time.

The predominant temper of modernism since the 1960s has shrunk from the exceptional, valuing only incremental change. The result is that art, rather than leading the formation of judgements, has tended to become the materialization of an industry (a "cultural industry" to be sure) based on norms that must not reach beyond the fashionably new.

Town has always sought the exceptional, in his own work and in his expectations of others. This is not a wish to be the exception that proves the rule, but rather the assertion that the only challenge is the extraordinary. The series of *Enigma* drawings of the 1960s, for instance, arose directly out of his frustrating recognition of a figure he was drawing as one he had done before. Hating to repeat himself is not some mania of self-ascribed virtuosity, but the rigorous self-criticism of an artist who imposes every challenge first on himself. The resulting series of drawings angrily exposes not simply the naturalness of human weakness but the perversion of power in the hands of moral and self-seeking mediocrity. On another level, in his *Tyranny of the Corner* series, he painted his rejection of the platitudes that sought to standardize the enterprise of painting. By this series of work he insisted that the activity of painting was not just symbolic of the activity of painting but an analogue for the complexity of human relations between freedom and order.

It is in this context that we must understand him saying, "I make up a set of rules and play within those rules until I win." The rules are neither arbitrary nor limited; they are made with an acute awareness of how the achievements of past art must be drawn into the challenge of the present. And he cannot accept the present as anything but dynamic and demanding; he cannot accept art as merely increments in an open-ended determinism. Robert Fulford wrote of Town in 1980:

He has developed at least a dozen different "manners," any one of which would have made the reputation of a less interesting artist. But he has insisted – rightly in my view – on displaying not just one narrow strip of his sensibility but the entire range.[1]

Enigma 1966
Brush, steel pen, black and white inks on grey paper

Criticism of Town's work has often fastened on to these shifts of "manners," and on to the fact that he has not encouraged a school of followers. Both complaints are tokens of a poverty of adventure and an inability to take the broad view that criticism properly demands. The challenge of art is the challenge of looking in order to think, not in order to confirm what is already known; and the challenge for young artists is to make their presence present. Of this Town has always been very clear, for himself and for others. Recently he said,

Why the hell should young artists pay any attention to us ? We're entirely comprised of the posts and slats in a fence they're trying to get over. We're immediate history, and there's nothing so terrible as immediate history.[2]

There can be no fault in seeking the exceptional; the fault lies in an art world more concerned with its stability than its valuations of art.

Stability, equated with the median, resists whatever and whomever is exceptional. Canadian reticence, at least towards its own heroes and heroines, is so well recorded as to be an article of national faith. Americans refuse to accept this of themselves, and the British assume the world's acceptance of their heroes and heroines. In Canada there is an assumption that to excel in one field may lead to arrogance, while to excel in several is a constitutional weakness. That Town has been a media personality, quoted and quotable, photographed and photogenic, has come to mean that the credit gained in those areas must be debited elsewhere. That his work through the 1970s, in particular the *Snaps* and *Parks* and *Toy Horses*, has not received the critical attention it demands is symptomatic more of a pervasive malaise than of an objective weighing of artistic merits.

The issue is not, however, simply a contrast between artist and public personality. Rather there are three aspects of a single force; the public personality is certainly one of them, but so is the sense of *making public*, and the *making public* arises from the intense and recluse-like existence of working. Town has not shrunk from stating his opinions – and they are never equivocal – nor has he failed to "put up." Whatever has been vital in his art and his writing he has set in the public arena. If he criticizes art that he sees around him, his own work is there to be seen in exhibition; if he criticizes the writing of others, his own writing is there to be read, in articles and, above all, in the texts he has written for *Enigmas, Silent Stars, Sound Stars, Film Stars, Albert Franck: Keeper of the Lanes*, and, with David Silcox, *Tom Thomson: The Silence and the Storm.*

In some essential ways the attempt to write a biography of Harold Town is rendered irrelevant by the very character of those contrasts among the public face, the making public, and the reclusive, painstaking compulsion to work. The point to be made by writing, rather than by only looking, is to approach the work as a whole, not as a series of disconnected moves – for they are not disconnected – nor as an attempt to read the standardizations of recent art history into his work. Rather the demands of writing are in seeking the unity behind the moves by approaching the work: facing it, not avoiding it; thinking about it, not indulging in pseudo-scientific psychologizing. We must look from the work into history, not the other way around. Rather than starting with a belief that Canadian art history should be written from the viewpoint of how individual artists match up to standards – invariably drawn from elsewhere – why not begin with the exceptional artist as an exception, and show how the exceptional can change our assumptions?

Tyranny of the Corner, Judge Set 1962
Oil and lucite on canvas

ONE

The activism of the *Automatistes* in Montreal during the 1940s and the Painters Eleven in Toronto a decade later, radically changed the course of art in Canada. Yet they were movements wholly distinct in motive, operation, and context. The *Automatistes*, led by Paul-Émile Borduas, were joined in the conviction that their collective voice manifested the potential freedom of a society repressed by custom, history, paternalism, and censorship. In this they retained something of the original revolutionary character of the avant-garde that Gabriel-Désiré Laverdant had asserted in 1845, "art as an instrument for social action and reform."[1] But despite the fundamental nature of the *Automatistes'* attack – an attack opposed with the force characteristic of institutions jealous and uncertain of their ground – and despite the energy it generated in artistic circles, advanced art in Montreal remained essentially an underground activity into the 1960s.

In contrast, from the mid-1950s, the Painters Eleven, united by their frustration with the art establishment, enjoyed a public profile, the support of writers in Toronto (in particular Pearl McCarthy and Robert Fulford), and an audience. They had a clear identity as "the new" that corresponded directly to the acknowledged changes within the society itself.

The *Automatistes* had both responded to and sought independence from the French Surrealist movement.[2] They were on the margins of the cultural debate in France, a nation defeated and divided by war and unstable in recovery; they sought freedom in Quebec, a homeland on the brink of major cultural and social change. Painters Eleven, formed ten years later, reflected a society building on the industrial expansion of Canada's wartime production and shifting its interests from Europe to closer economic and cultural relations with the United States. The point of cultural reference in Toronto, a city growing rapidly in population and economic power,[3] was New York, which by the 1950s, was the dominant centre of western art.[4] The quantity and consistency of attention that Toronto artists received in the 1950s and 1960s arose in recognition of their relevance; that of their colleagues in Quebec, however, occurred as the stubborn insistence of a few writers and editors to press the claims of an artistic underground.

The distinctions between Montreal and Toronto were described in the 1950s by Rodolphe de Repentigny, perhaps the most perceptive critic of his day. He pointed out how each new artistic movement in Quebec entered into the "ideological and social upheaval," whereas in Toronto there was no urge to relate art movements to an intellectual identity [*communauté*]. Toronto artists were not seeking to revolutionize the plastic arts, but rather "to live fully their own time."[5]

The value of Painters Eleven and its purpose was quite different from that of the *Automatistes* or from *Les Plasticiens*, a group formed and led by Repentigny in Montreal during the mid-1950s. There was no formal leadership, and there was no common or declared theoretical pursuit. But it is too narrow a view to declare, as was suggested at the time, that Painters Eleven was not an artistic movement because it had not published a manifesto. Its existence as a movement was the dynamics of its collective opposition to the turgid status quo. The measure of its success was the change it forced by opening perspectives onto the broader cultural issues.

It was indicative of the situation in Toronto that it should have been those eleven artists who in November 1953 agreed to exhibit together. The members of the group ranged widely in age, experience, talent, and ambition. They were linked by their interests in and concerns with the art of their own time (although in this they were not alone among artists in the area) and united in their frustration at not being able to show their work in a meaningful way. The art societies, conservative in attitude and organization, controlled the most significant opportunities for public exhibition, and the small number and limited range of private galleries offered no viable alternative.

The group recognized that their collective effort could gain what it was all but impossible to achieve individually. In their decision to act together, however, they specifically denied a common aesthetic direction. Their action was radical in the context of Canadian art, but it was not revolutionary: it did not collectively seek the destruction of existing institutions. Harold Town wrote for the group, "We paint the way we have to paint. We have no axe to grind with traditionalists. Nobody is forced to look at our paintings. All we want to do is create to the best of our ability."[6] And indeed, the Eleven continued to show with the Ontario Society of Artists, the Royal Canadian Academy and other societies.[7] Their demand was for a freedom of place.

This ambivalence toward the societies may appear curious, but it reflects a situation more fluid than that of a uniform establishment against which the *refusées* could rebel. The most celebrated resignations from the OSA had come two and a half years before the formation of Painters Eleven: in March 1951, four senior members resigned over the jury's selection of "modern art" for the 79th Annual Exhibition. One complained of "just plain ugliness,"[8] but Kenneth Forbes, the most vocal and outraged of the four, objected to "abstractionists" (Jock Macdonald and R. York Wilson were among the jurors) being allowed "to judge the work of the rationalists."[9] He claimed that there was a conspiracy afoot as galleries all over the world were being filled with abstract art, "most of it done in factories." But most fascinating and most telling, in the context of Toronto in the early fifties, was his assuming a high moral tone in defence of the Protestant work ethic. People, he said, who made their own money did not go after "modernistic art"; only those who depended on inherited wealth did.

However, he was not leading a monolithic opposition to the new; William Winter, an ex-president of the OSA, welcomed the jury's choices; A.Y. Jackson, who both embodied and symbolized the orthodox direction of Canadian painting, entered the lists: "We broke from old traditions and now we are old tradition. I am an objective painter, I should like to go abstract, but I don't know how."[10] Forbes continued to fulminate – he was convinced Canada would become a laughingstock at the 1958 Brussels World Fair for including modernistic work in its official exhibition (for that, he drew a classic Town rejoinder, "I'm so glad to hear from Kenneth Forbes. I thought he was dead, but I only had his pictures to judge by") – but the debate was empty.

But despite the limited exhibition opportunities and the severe difficulty of making a career in art (Town, for example, was thirty when he first sold a picture), the time was ripe for change. The Painters Eleven group, because of its varied membership and its spirited controversy not only in advocating modernism but also in its widely reported internal disagreements, represented that time and its potential. It represented a desire for change and the differences within a society just beginning to recognize its pluralism.

Although the group existed for seven years, its essential collective effort was expended during the first three years. After that, with the gradual expansion of commercial galleries, with the growth of an audience, and with a profile for the new raised by the press, individual rather than collective efforts became dominant. The group, in any case, was never a close-knit unit. From its foundation in November 1953 to its dissolution on October 19, 1960, nineteen meetings took place: nine in 1956 and five in 1958, the two most active years for the group's exhibitions.[11] Moreover, it was rare that the whole membership was present at a meeting. By 1957 its number had been reduced, first by Oscar Cahén's death the previous November, then by William Ronald's resignation and, effectively, by Ray Mead's move to Montreal.[12] Both Alexandra Luke and Jock Macdonald felt that the 1958 exhibition at the Park Gallery should be the group's last.[13] There was no exhibition in 1959 and the two museum exhibitions held in 1960 had more the character of retrospectives than radical attacks.[14]

The generally positive reaction of American artists and critics to the group show with the American Abstract Artists Association at the Riverside Museum in New York in 1956 was a watershed. Thereafter the tensions within the group – of personality, of principle, of ambition – broke open. Ronald, who had been living in New York since 1954, and with the particular support of Macdonald, was pressing the claims for wider attention of the group. In May 1957 he proposed inviting the critic Clement Greenberg to visit the artists in Toronto. Greenberg agreed on the condition that the artists pay his expenses. Town and Walter Yarwood refused to participate. Of the seven artists who took part, reactions to the critic's comments were mixed: Ray Mead, Macdonald, and Luke found them valuable and supportive (Macdonald's initial enthusiasm for the critic's opinion later cooled), Jack Bush was deeply impressed by what Greenberg had to say.[15]

In retrospect the Greenberg visit can be seen as having put focus on the differing ambitions and directions in the group, differences that have been echoed among successive generations of artists. Ronald (encouraged by Macdonald) had already made his choice by moving to New York; he remained in the United States until 1967. Bush accepted the centrality of New York in a different way. Although he continued to work in Toronto, he built close friendships with Greenberg and with such artists as Kenneth Noland and Jules Olitski, whose work led the mainstream of painting through the 1960s. He wanted his work to meet the challenge of what he considered the major painting of his time, a challenge that carried with it the certainty of modernism's continuity. The approach that he took has been followed by many other painters not only in Toronto but elsewhere in the country, most notably in Edmonton and Saskatoon. Bush was attacked for his compliance to the "Greenberg line," attacks encouraged in the later 1960s and early 1970s by a wave of anti-American nationalism.[16] But Bush's influence on younger Toronto artists from the late 1960s was of major importance; it has had a real effect on the shape and temper of art in Toronto.

Harold Town's position has been distinctly different from those of both Ronald and Bush. It is analogous to the contrasts within the structure of his work – open to the achievement of past art, but grounded in the vital reality of working in and from one place. It is, given the peculiar twists of art world opinion, a position many have found difficult to accept. On the one hand he has been criticized, in what amounts to an accusation of failure of nerve, for being provincial, for not testing himself in a larger artistic field. (This accusation overlooks all his exhibitions in many parts of the world.) Others have dismissed his determination to maintain his independence by working in Toronto as inauthentic, "the saleable cultural-nationalist poses of an artist who is really a sellout [to American cultural interests]."[17]

Views such as these (setting aside those based on clashes of personality) arise either from doctrinaire political stances or from a failure to recognize the substantial issues that determine the complex character of art at a particular time in a particular place. The breakthrough made by the Painters Eleven as a group was not accidental but symptomatic of a broader process of cultural questioning and self-examination, a process first formalized by the establishment of the Federation of Canadian Artists at the Kingston Conference of 1941 and the Massey Commission Report a decade later.

Still, in the 1950s, artistic issues continued to be judged by cultural terms already overtaken by events. "Progress" was still measured in the narrow terms of schools or styles, as if any thought of modernism in Canada had to be gauged according to its degree of continuity with the Group of Seven. One critic reviewing the Painters Eleven in 1957 found that they were not the originators of a "Canadian" style, and that their references to American Abstract Expressionism would lead to a dead end. In short, rather than betting on the enduring character of the Group of Seven, they had backed the wrong stylistic horse:

The appeal of this style will not be great, or lasting, and some of the Painters Eleven know it…a flight into abstraction…is not after all a release for the human imagination.[18]

Aside from the fact that our capacity of imagination exists because of our capacity for abstraction, such an opinion misreads the relationship between a style and a culture. It is a misreading that continues every time "the new" is asserted without a full regard for history and by negating the complexity of the existing context. But the relatively rapid growth of attention given to the Painters Eleven beginning in 1954 – the excitement they generated, the anger they raised – happened not only because they advocated artistic modernism, but also because the tensions among the members of the group asserted the broader and pluralistic issues of a changing society: ultimately the best art to come out of Painters Eleven was in the work of Town, Bush, and Ronald, three artists wholly divergent in approach and context.

Ronald, and later Bush, developed pictorial languages that must be read within the context of mainstream American art, their individuality is identifiable within the broad movement of modernism, and the effects can be traced in several generations of Toronto artists. Town's work, however, is dominated by individuality in subject matter and by an approach to style and formal decision-making defined by the variety of that individuality. His is an artistic character that defies the desire to define work in terms of a "norm" sought by many critics as a way to rationalize and contain individual expression.

Freed from the assumptions that tethered judgements in Toronto, de Repentigny properly recognized the character of Town's work. Reviewing Town's exhibition of single autographic prints at Guido Molinari's Galerie L'Actuelle in March 1957, Repentigny wrote

An artist who acquires an extraordinarily varied skill is not particularly rare. That he knows what to do with it is much rarer. Harold Town, a painter from Toronto, is one of these artists who, in Canada, can be counted on one's fingers.[19]

What is valuable is not simply the responsiveness of an individual to the variety of his experiences, but his ability to absorb experience common to all and subsume it in uncommon expression.

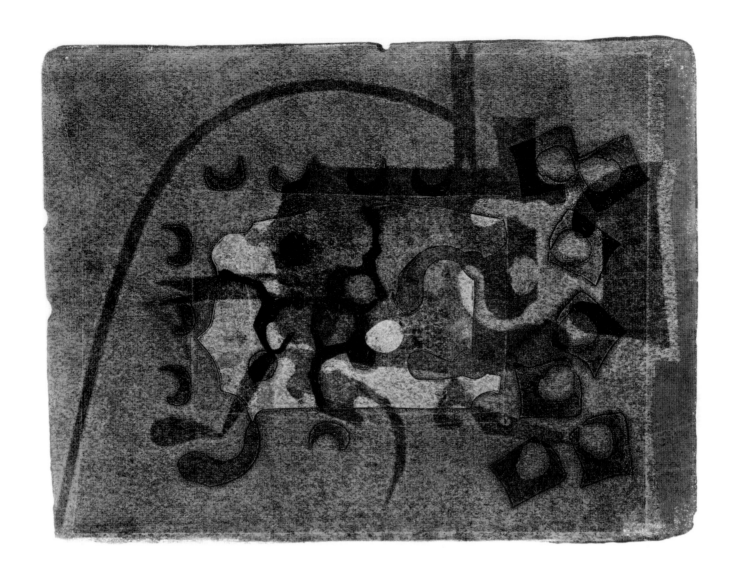

The First Infernal Submarine 1957
Single Autographic Print

TWO

The opening of the first Painters Eleven exhibition at the Roberts Gallery brought out "huge crowds" that February evening in 1954. It had been preceded by strong advance publicity, particularly on television, but who knows what expectations this had raised. Curiosity? Smug outrage at what was happening to the erstwhile dependable reputation of the Roberts Gallery? A desire to be irritated by something new? The hopes the group may have had were matched by its naiveté, a naiveté reflecting the differences between the expediency of collective action and a move toward individual freedom, between painting as one wished and sustaining a career while doing so.

There was little by way of sales – a few works on paper were bought – and of the reviews only Pearl McCarthy's came close to recognizing what the exhibition meant:

...there are great differences of temperament and approach, and this collection will best be appraised by leaving aside all debate on the merits of representational versus abstract art and looking at these pictures for what they are. So long as artists do not claim to have the sole answer to what-is-art, they should be appreciated strictly in terms of what they are seeking to do.[1]

"Modernistic art" by local painters had, of course, been shown in Toronto before,[2] but the notion of a group, however loosely based, devoted to modernism was new and gave a greater sense of unity than the work warranted.

For their next show, at Roberts Gallery the following year, the group produced a brochure containing a statement written by Town on behalf of the group (he was the author of all the group's "official" statements) that explicitly disclaimed a common theoretical base:

There is no manifesto here for the times. By now there is little harmony in the noticeable disagreement. But there is a profound regard for the consequences of our complete freedom."[3]

Nevertheless, in the absence of a broader critical context, there was an *appearance* of unity, if only in the dominance of strong colour, abstract forms, and the puzzling relation between the paintings' titles and what they looked like. The exhibitions were experiences for which the inclusion of some abstract pictures in the amorphous mass of the Ontario Society of Artists exhibitions had been no preparation. It is significant that at no time during the Painters Eleven's existence did the group hold an exhibition at the Art Gallery of Toronto. Exhibitions in Toronto (apart from the two touring shows at Hart House and a small show at the Arts and Letters Club) were held at commercial galleries; but the group did show in public galleries from Montreal to Vancouver and also in New York and Dallas.

Town has long insisted that communal feeling within the group was

Essence of Rex 1953
Oil on masonite

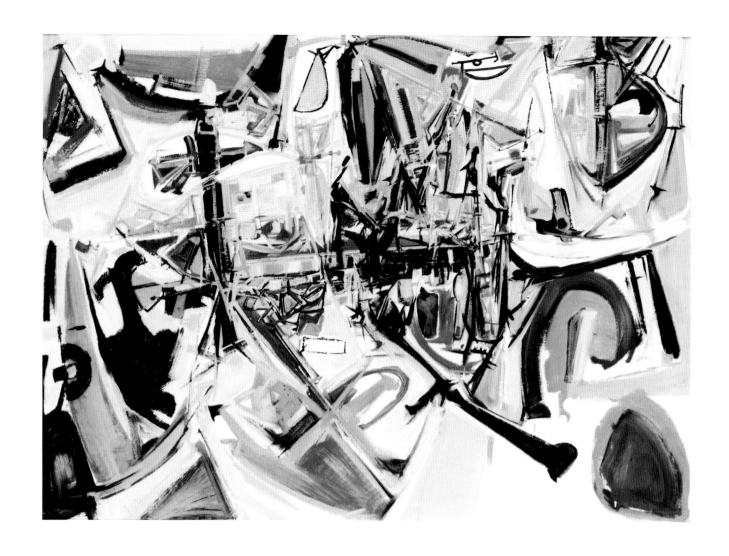

Mechanical Forest Sound 1953
Oil on masonite

"slight"; he believes the group had no influence on his own work nor on that of Ronald or Yarwood.[4] This seems to support the often repeated charge of arrogance regarding his "claims to originality."[5] But it has often been attested that the group really comprised a series of personal friendships. And the statements issued by the group insisted *from the start* the primacy of individuality (coming from Town's pen and reflecting his point of view). Most important, however, is the evidence provided by his work. As I will show, the essential interests, the diversity, and critical directions that form the foundations of his work were firmly set down during the 1950s. The character of what was achieved then lay more outside the aesthetic concerns of the group than in concert with them.

Town showed three paintings at the first Painters Eleven exhibition: *Tumult for a King, Essence of Rex* (Ill. p. 27), and *Conversation between Clowns* (Ill. p. 33). These paintings, as many others of the same period such as *Mechanical Forest Sound* (Ill. p. 28), are marked by aggressive colour and a density in drawing and incident. Brilliant reds and oranges are juxtaposed; drawing is done with paint squeezed directly from the tube, and every part of the surface is filled with painterly activity that develops a complex, almost labyrinthine interweaving of spatial illusions. Yet these three pictures present distinct references. *Mechanical Forest Sound*, its surface fragmented into cells of colour, refers to the displays of neon lights in downtown Toronto, not simply as an impression but imaginatively, the way a man from ancient Egypt might find them "an overwhelming mystery."[6] It is like a mirror in the present of the mystery we find in the past; the impact of difference is more vital than the detailed interpretations of signs and their context. *Essence of Rex* is related to *Monument to a Politician* 1956 (Ill. p. 30) and *Uneasy Emperor* 1960, but where these two caricature people raised up in self-importance, *Essence of Rex* reflects Town's delight in unpretentious and spontaneous responses to his pictures. A seven-year-old boy, Rex Hagan, brought Marshall McLuhan's daughter to look at Town's work. Rex's pronouncement "It's not very good, is it . . . ." to one of the pictures Town showed them prompted the painting *Essence of Rex*, dedicated to his young critic. *Conversation between Clowns* appears self-reflexive, the outward challenge of the artist – clowns do not converse so much as shout and declaim – that covers the private monologue.

In the 1954 Canadian Group of Painters exhibition at the Art Gallery of Toronto, Town showed *Morning Alarm* (1953-54) (Ill. p. 31). Here the challenge and certainly the choice to exhibit this painting was matched to the circumstances in which it was shown. It is essentially an urban picture, compressed in space, active throughout, one area breaking rudely into another, allowing no rest or escape. It was the right painting for the Canadian Group of Painters, the designated successors to the Group of Seven, who had declared the northern landscape essential to the character of Canadian art.

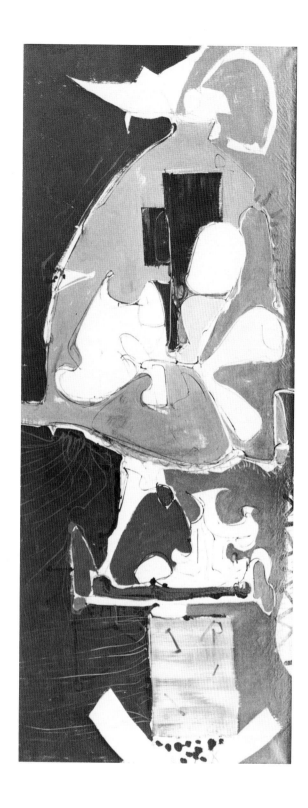

Monument to a Politician 1956
Oil and lucite on canvas

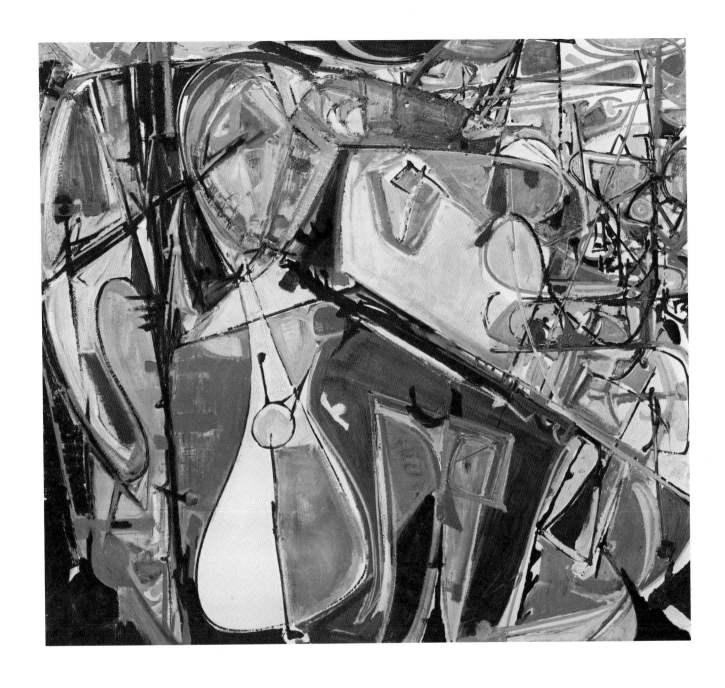

Morning Alarm 1953-54
Oil on masonite

At one level these pictures are concerned with challenging both the conventions of painting at the time and the work of his colleagues. But what is also clear, when we consider the drawings and prints he was making at the same time, is the paradigm of his approach. He has described himself as being unable to separate the past from the present, and the present from the future. Throughout his career his work has been a complex generation and interweaving of ideas, memories, reactions, and techniques reflecting the circumstances of his time and place, drawing in history, and reaching forward in imaginative speculation.

In 1954 Town held his first one-man exhibition. It took place at Douglas Duncan's Picture Loan Society and comprised the first showing of his single autographic prints. The prints, a remarkable series of unique works he began in late 1953 and stopped making in 1959, were distinct from any of the work being done around him. They had nothing to do with the painterly concerns projected through the Painters Eleven exhibitions, and it was through them, more than any other aspect of his work, that his independence was first marked and recognized in Canada and abroad.

It is no coincidence that in 1954, that year of the initial critical impact of Painters Eleven, Town was already defining and asserting his independence. This is clear in the range of his work and its references; in his simultaneous work on paintings, drawings, and prints, in his development of formal structures appropriate to those media, and by their quite distinct ranges in subject and style. There are, of course, interrelations in themes and crossovers from one technique to another, but two elements were clear then and have remained unchanged. First, there is no hierarchy in his work: one approach or technique is never subordinated to another. Second, each work, in whatever medium, is begun and pursued as a complete and independent statement. He does not, for instance, make drawings as sketches for paintings. Each drawing, like each painting, each print and each collage has a unique subject and pictorial expression.

Yet another contrasting factor is apparent in the work from 1954. With the single autographic prints we first see Town's practice of working through series. A series may arise from a particular technique, from a subject theme, or from the pursuit of a pictorial issue. They may comprise a small number of works on a single theme such as the *Deadboat Pond* paintings of 1956-57 or a large group done within a short period of time, such as the *Tyranny of the Corner* paintings of 1962 and 1963 (p. 19 and pp. 106-107) that were concerned with one particular pictorial issue. Other series are worked on over long periods of time: he made many hundreds of single autographic prints during a period of five years; and the *Toy Horse* series (frontispiece and pp. 181-185), for which he made over seven hundred individual works, occupied him for seven years.

The patterns of work that describe Town's career were in essence formed by 1954 and only in part engaged with the group interests of Painters

Conversation Between Clowns 1953
Oil on masonite

Eleven. He expressed this indirectly in 1958 writing on behalf of the group about the recognition they had gained:

…we have secured recognition for the vital, creative painting being done in this province. In this sense our work [as a group] will soon be accomplished, and no doubt we will return to the singular ways that are best for painters, anywhere, anytime.[7]

For Town, in significant respects, it was not a matter of a "return" but rather a continuation of "singular ways" already defined.

The artists of the Painters Eleven group to whom Town was closest were Yarwood and Oscar Cahén. Town met Cahén in 1946 or 1947, when both men were working as commercial artists. Cahén often spoke to Town of Yarwood and, later, when Cahén and Yarwood were working together in the Wellington Building, he introduced Town to Yarwood. Cahén, who was eight years older than Town, was quickly establishing a substantial reputation and a successful career as an illustrator.[8] In November 1956, at the age of forty, Cahén was killed in a car accident. Three years later, Town and Yarwood organized a memorial exhibition of Cahén's work, for which Town wrote a sensitive appreciation. The exhibition was included

Oscar Cahén
Vivid Structure
Oil on masonite

as a special section of the 87th Annual Exhibition of the Ontario Society of Artists.

Cahén's influence on his Painters Eleven colleagues has often been described. Bush, Mead and, above all, Tom Hodgson have acknowledged their debt. But despite some claims that Cahén arrived in Canada a fully fledged painter,[9] his earliest paintings support Town's contention that Cahén's serious work as a painter resulted from his contact with Yarwood.[10] There is, it seems, a spirit of challenge between the paintings of Town and those of Cahén from 1953 to 1956, a challenge in strength of colour, in the relationship of figuration and abstraction, and in the desire for the monumental. I say challenge because the temper of their work is distinct, as can be seen in a comparison between Town's *Essence of Rex* (Ill. p. 27) and Cahén's *Vivid Structure* (fig. p. 34), two paintings close in date.[11]

There are similarities: in the compression of incident, in the spatial division of the surface by complex shaping, and in overpainting to form contrasts of painterly texture. For Cahén, however, drawing remains more tightly held to the definition of form and this traditional character is emphasized by the figure being set within a space described by a horizon or ground line. Town, on the other hand, activates the surface by lines and, through their all-over emphasis, he integrates the whole surface rather than dividing it between a figure set against a ground. We must go back to earlier works of Town's, like the *Side Show Performer* of 1950 (Ill. p. 35), to find a similar division in spatial structure and his move toward an integrated surface was already implicit by 1950-51 in a series of paintings on characters from Cervantes, for instance, *Sancho, Don Quixote and Rocinante* (Ill. p. 39), that are built up on a cellular structure of lines and planes.

At this time Cahén was strongly impressed with the work of the American artist Abraham Rattner and the English artist Graham Sutherland. In works that Cahén was making around 1951 the influence of Sutherland's spiky, surrealistic abstractions is clearly evident. Although there was little contemporary American work in Toronto at that time, English contemporary art was being bought by the Women's Committee of the Art Gallery of Toronto; pictures by Sutherland, Ben Nicholson, Peter Lanyon, and Ceri Richards entered the collection in the early 1950s.

In 1956 Town made a substantial group of paintings on eight-by-four-foot sheets of masonite that, if not as successful as *Fall of Babylon* (Ill. p. 36) and the *Deadboat Pond* pictures, were ambitious in their scale and the attack of their colour drawing. The last works of Cahén, varied in direction and punchy in colour, still retain a more measured structure. Town's paintings of the time had a restlessness, even a violence, as if he was wanting to subvert the very structure from which he had worked, the structure that had brought his and Cahén's work close together in the early 1950s.

The relationship between the two men and their work overlies a broader

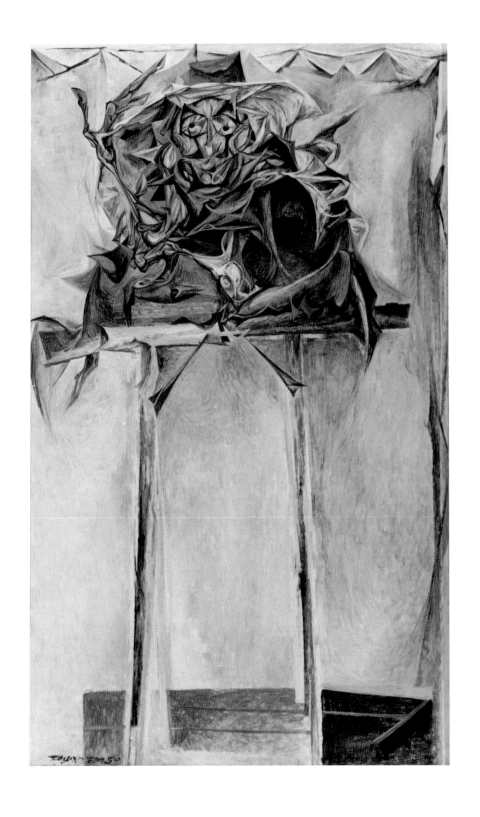

Side Show Performer 1950
Oil on masonite

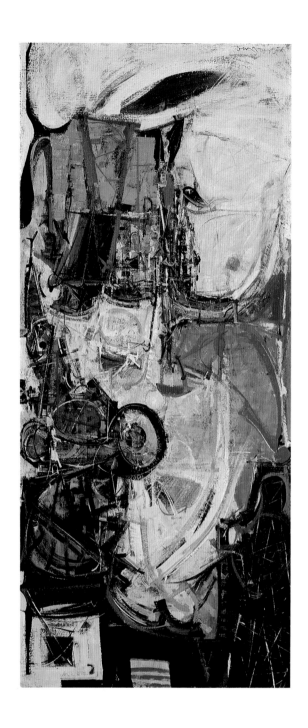

Fall of Babylon 1956
Oil and lucite on canvas

Garden for Eurasian Princess 1957-58
Collage

and more complex issue: the relation of the assertion of individuality and the historical assessment of the development of art. As I have mentioned, Town had set out by 1954 the terms of his work: its concern with a range of subjects, styles, and media; the practice of working in series; and the integrity of each work of art in whatever medium. These decisions could only be determined individually and pursued within the studio. But the sense of aggression, of competition, demanded its own outlets. He had not at this time "gone public" – it was only in the late 1950s that he agreed to demands for interviews. If the competitiveness was in art making it could only be with the members of Painters Eleven, and among them the real challenge could only come from Cahén – successful, urbane, admired by those who came in contact with him, with a range of experience unmatched by others in the group.

This tension between the inner decisions of work and their outward projection is raised implicitly by two very different assessments of Town during that period. In 1971 Robert Fulford wrote:

… Town has tended to feel the character of his period intensely and reflects it in his work. He isn't an artist who can be seen exclusively in terms of art history…in the 1950s he was a leader in Canada…of art's heroic effort to save us all from boring ourselves to death.[12]

More recently Barrie Hale has recalled Fulford's opinion but has argued that Town was not unique in "feeling intensely what he perceives the character of his period to be," and that, rather than saving us from boredom, his heroic effort is to be himself: "all the rest *is* art history." He compares Town's paintings, prints, and collages of the 1950s to the work of his Painters Eleven colleagues. "For all the attack of their disparate elements, Town's pictures of the Painters Eleven period do not often partake of the painterly fibre of, say, Hodgson's, Yarwood's, Ronald's, and even Bush's."[13]

The distinction here is important in general terms, and crucial to the assessment of Town. Fulford sets the acts of the individual in relation to *art* as the point of engagement to reveal his time and place; Hale subsumes individuality in the drive of modernism's progress, that in this case relates to the orthodox radicalism of the time, New York Abstract Expressionism. "Painterly fibre" in this sense is not an absolute value but a measure of recent art history arising from New York. To exemplify this point Hale suggests some comparisons between specific works of Town with those of his colleagues, in every case but one, between a Town print or collage and a painting by one of the other artists. By this he sets to the margins the individual fibre of Town's work, but allows the individuality of the other artists to exist only in their conformity to the dominant art history of the time.

Town has described how from 1953 to 1956 he was "…mainly concerned with printmaking" and from 1957 to 1960 "divided my time equally between painting and collage."[14] From this the implication has been drawn that he avoided the challenge of the most advanced art coming from New York, which was concerned almost wholly with painting. But the issue can – and I believe should – be set differently. The challenge was not in seeking a measure of individuality while conforming to the mainstream but in achieving critical individuality. The real value of Painters Eleven as a group was twofold: between 1954 and 1957 its collective strength freed the potential individuality in its members; under the arts society system, it would have taken much longer to achieve. Second, its critical attack lay initially not in trying to approximate New York but in breaking open the patterns of artistic behaviour established in Toronto. The success of the show at New York's Riverside Museum in 1956 did not lie in any pretense of shifting opinion in New York but rather in the claim the group could press in Toronto. And as the unity of the group diminished after 1957 (its diversity could not be bound together forever) it was, at least implicitly, in recognition of the fact that any future artistic value they could achieve depended on the artists standing up to be counted individually.

Town did not make prints and collages to avoid the challenge of painting. He continued to paint, but he had to work from within his own terms; everything he did bore on the singularity of expression. From the perspective of the early 1960s the stature, the density, and the individuality that marked Town's work was unprecedented. And the reception of his work in Toronto and at the exhibitions he held in New York was strikingly positive. The symbol of this in popular terms was his one-man exhibition at the Laing Galleries in 1961: people lined up outside the door and arguments broke out over the right to acquire certain pictures. This occasion, with its attendant lunacy, was the centre of a brief but significant boom for acquiring contemporary Canadian art. Still, the fact is that in 1961 Town had an incomparable body of paintings, prints, collages, and drawings.

It was an extraordinary complex and independent body of work to which there was no challenge in Toronto. Of his Painters Eleven colleagues, Ronald, living in the United States, held all but one of his solo shows between 1957 and 1962 at the Kootz Gallery in New York;[15] by 1960 Yarwood had all but stopped painting to sculpt; Bush was just beginning to "hit his stride"; Hodgson, after the brilliant attack of his works in the mid and later 1950s, changed emphasis and showed infrequently; Mead became involved in the concerns of Montreal abstraction and for seven years from 1963 to 1969 did no painting.[16]

Sancho, Don Quixote and Rosinante 1949-50
Oil on masonite

Neons at Noon 1954
Oil on masonite

Gateway to Atlantis No. 2 1957
Single Autographic Print

Three Musicians 1949-50
Oil on masonite

The Window in the Studio 1952
Oil on masonite

Monument to an Unpublished Poet 1958
Single Autographic Print

Radar Detecting Winter
Single Autographic Print

THREE

In December 1953 Town made the first of the single autographic prints. From Oscar Cahén he had bought an old lithographic press with a Bavarian limestone approximately twenty by sixteen inches. During the next five years Town made hundreds, perhaps even thousands, of prints on this press.[1] Until 1956 while he was living on St. Mary Street, he worked in extremely cramped and even dangerous conditions in a basement. The ceiling was so low in the press area that he resorted to wearing first a toque stuffed with tissue and later a football helmet to protect himself against constantly banging into a wooden ceiling beam. He had, however, no protection from the fumes of the inks and solvents, and the lack of proper ventilation led to a serious lung problem.

His working conditions were improved when he moved to Rathnally Avenue and installed the press in the attic. He moved to his Castle Frank Crescent home in 1959 and again put the press in the basement. At that time he stopped the series because, as he has said, the prints had become so popular, but he continued to use the press for etchings. When he first showed the prints in 1954 they had aroused little interest; but this changed markedly by 1957, in no small way due to the attention he received in international exhibitions. His prints were shown at the 1956 Venice Biennale; in 1957, at Ljubljana, Yugoslavia, the Milan Triennial and the São Paulo Biennial; in 1958, at Lugano and Grenchen, Switzerland. He was awarded prizes at Ljubljana, São Paulo, and Lugano. Once again it was the familiar story of outside interest legitimizing Canadian recognition.

Stopping work on the prints in 1959 was not, perhaps, only to counter their popularity but also an unwillingness to be known only as a printmaker. The potential for invention of his techniques were by no means exhausted and he has subsequently regretted closing off their further possibilities. They now have a classic sense, representative of their time yet without precedent or successors and, embodying the essential independence of his work, they set the aesthetic character and the inventive and technical procedures for the future.

From the start the works in the series were made as monotypes or, as he designated them, "single autographic prints." It is rare for an artist to make so large a number of monotypes. Rare, too, to use a lithographic press, which was developed specifically to allow artists and commercial designers to produce very large editions of the same image. The whole process and the large amount of time given to an individual print cut across the grain. This is significant in view of the fact that in the early 1950s, Town, and a number of his Painters Eleven colleagues - Cahén, Yarwood, Bush, Hodgson, Mead - were doing commercial art. Town set himself both against the commercial and traditional art uses of lithography: he used multiple colours, not with several stones but with a single one; he drew with resist, drew from the reverse, impressed a wide range of materials onto the surfaces - card, paper, string, leather, felt - and in some cases collaged materials to the print. He developed surface textures and spatial illusions that have no peer.

The prints established the individuality of Town's work through procedures of contrast between the additive character in an individual work and the multiplicity of extending the technical and formal inventions into a series. In terms of that process, both technical and inventive, the single autographic prints and the collages of the later 1950s are closely related. In many of the collages, for instance *Dream of the Samurai* (Ill. p. 49), *Garden for Eurasian Princess* (Ill. p. 37), and *Monument to C.T. Currelly* (Ill. p. 75), he used prints or fragments of prints as major collage elements. Yet this interrelationship in materials and techniques goes far beyond simple formal devices.

In the most basic sense "collage" describes a technique, pasting or gluing materials to a surface. By extension it also refers to a means of public declaration, *collage d'affiches*, meaning posting bills or notices. This sense of publication carries, as well, the implication of being against convention, even illegitimate: in, for example, the pejorative phrase, *c'est un collage* meaning "they're having an affair." The Cubist collages of Braque and Picasso broke the conventions of pictorial illusion; the photomontage of Raoul Hausmann and George Grosz were statements of political dissent. The critical function of collage was further extended by Kurt Schwitters; in 1944 Herbert Read wrote of Schwitters' "deep protest against the chromium-plated conception of modernism."[2]

Town's use of collage – and by this I refer also to the additive, layering process of his printmaking that leads towards collage construction – is a declaration of dissent, and an assertion of private imagery. The collages express not only a general sense of opposition to painterly convention but also a denial of the specific concerns of advanced art as they were understood in Toronto in the mid-1950s. (Was it only coincidence that Town's first large-scale collages date from 1957, the year of Clement Greenberg's first visit to Toronto?)

But if collage has long carried the force of dissent, it also imposes, against tradition, an alternative structure for the relationship between perception and expression. Meyer Schapiro has related collage to the tradition of still-life painting, and to the control over the material environment and to the construction of interests other than the strictly pictorial. He described it as expressing

… an empirical standpoint wherein our knowledge of proximate objects… [objects close at hand and smaller than ourselves] is the model or ground of all knowledge… 'the reality of what we can see is what we can handle.'[3]

This contrast – of collage as dissent and collage as a structure of control emanating from "an empirical standpoint" – expands to other levels of contrast. Collage is, in Town's usage, reaching out for scattered, impersonal, and discarded materials to enclose them in the subjective unity of art. And

Radar Detecting Spring 1959
Single Autographic Print

Dream of the Samurai 1957
Collage

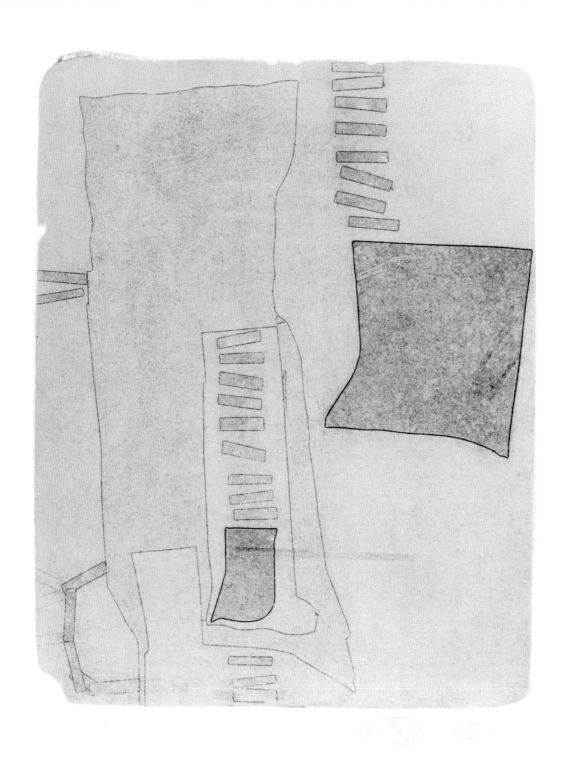

Up and Down 1954
Single Autographic Print

that subjective unity is given objectivity by the transformations of the materials in art. The multiplicity of personal experience – reflected in the multiple colours and shapes of the collage materials – is compressed to the economy of art, and by that to the potential of images for meaning. Yet it is an economy that opens a range of invention, whether in the technique of printmaking or in the use of the pencil line in his recent drawings, *The Famous* (Ill. p. 9 and pp. 204-211). It is the same economy that reveals the potential in other artifacts, such as the child's toy that initiated the *Toy Horse* series (Ill. frontispiece and pp. 181-185) or Florence Vale's *Pyramid of Roses* drawing that led to his *Vale Variations* series.

Collage is at the heart of Town's work – not simply as a technique or a style or a temporary means to clarify ideas, but as a complex, multi-directional interweaving of technique, materials, experience, and expression. To look at his work only in the anaemic vein in which modernism is often described – stylistic novelty, solutions to pictorial "problems," approximations to perceived movements of the progressive – is not only to overlook his work, but to fail to recognize his responses to the circumstances of the time surrounding him.

The single autographic prints comprised his first extended group of works that fully engaged these contrasts of transformation: a multiple technique used for unique purposes, a flat surface forced to bear the impressions of multiple processes. And from that derives the potential of simple material forms to be transformed into images of the natural world, into signs and totems, into historical and mythological speculations, into all the observations, memories, and perceptions that are his to transform.

The earliest single autographic prints were simple linear structures using a limited range of colours; black forms and, perhaps, one additional colour. The forms themselves tended to describe separate units of shape or simple overlappings; yet they quickly developed, even within such limitations, the elegance and discipline of his early drawings. *Up and Down* (Ill. p. 50), done a few months into the series, refers to the movement of elevators in a building, and the print reflects these reciprocating balances. This simple print contrasts to the paintings of the time – *Neons at Noon* (Ill. p. 40), for instance – with their densely packed forms and strident colours. But Town rapidly realized the potential of the printing technique, and the prints develop such complex relations between shape and structure, colour and texture, illusion and subject matter, that not only was their own potential expanded, but they opened up a range of possibilities taken up in the paintings of the late 1950s and 1960s.

As he expanded the number of colours in a print and integrated not only drawn elements, but shapes printed from a variety of materials, the prints took on a special density held between the compression within the print – layer on layer of coloured inks, overlays of printed forms – and the potential for illusion in the textures and optical spatial separations within the colour.

Totem for Tinker 1958
Single Autographic Print

Memory of High Park 1957-58
Single Autographic Print

The very character of the prints seems to run counter to the expectations of contemporary advanced painting. Whereas the autographic character of the paintings lay in the handwriting of the gesture bringing the soul-searching to the surface in broad sweeps and slashes, Town's prints compressed personal memory and experience from the fragments of printed material. They present a dark and intimate world, suggestive in title, and filled with curious signs simultaneously personal and historical, that demand interpretation like archaeological finds layered in time.

The prints, in their subject matter and imaginative process, come from direct personal experience, from childhood memories, or from historical re-creations. Yet in developing their own iconographic world of the print, they reflect such complexity that "the real, the potential, the merely possible, the entirely imagined blend and merge together to the extent that even the author would have difficulty in distinguishing them."[4]

The references in the prints range from Greek mythology to Canadian history and topography. *Gateway to Atlantis* (Ill. pp. 41 and 68) recalls the mythological lost land; *Festival of Lemuria* (Ill. p. 55) refers to a Roman springtime festival when the spirits of the dead visited, and people threw black beans to exorcise the evil spirits, chanting "Ghosts of my fathers, go out"; *Bridge over the Lethe* refers to the river of Hades which brings forgetfulness of all that was said and done in life. *The Curve at Clandeboye* recalls the times when Town went to watch Tom Hodgson, a member of Canada's Olympic paddling team, training on a canal at the Toronto Islands, and *Symbol for Poundmaker* (Ill. p. 56) is a tribute to a Cree chief who, convicted of treason-felony for his part in the North West Rebellion of 1885, died within weeks of his release from jail. Yet another level of metaphor is introduced by *Machine of Cagliostro* (Ill. p. 57), referring to the actions – the machinations – of the notorious eighteenth-century swindler Guiseppe Balsamo, alias Count Alessandro di Cagliostro who, among his other scams, offered for sale the secret of everlasting youth.[5]

Another group of prints refers to Oriental figures and themes – to the brilliant and politically manipulative Chinese courtesan in *The Aura of Yang-Kue-Fei*, and to Japanese history in *The Place of the Samurai*. The explicit titles are Town's acknowledgement of the spatial construction and illusion by texture in Oriental art. There is, for instance, in the spareness and delicate precision of *Monument to an Unpublished Poet* (Ill. p. 44), something of the character of a Haiku;[6] this is a rigorously disciplined poetic form dependent on a few images that must include a reference to the natural world, and a sense of feeling left open to the imagination. In Town's rendering a fruit-like form, extending into a schematized hand holding two leaves, is reflected and enlarged like a shadow. *The Place of the Samurai* intuitively responds to a Japanese sense of narrative, wherein the reality of action arises from propitious meetings between human activity and the natural environment. This is different from the traditional western sense

Festival of Lemuria 1957
Single Autographic Print

Symbol for Poundmaker 1958
Single Autographic Print

Machine of Cagliostro 1957-58
Single Autographic Print

Pyre of Celestial Parts 1956
Single Autographic Print

The Meeting
Single Autographic Print

of narrative in which the illusion of a seamless environment encloses human actions.

Town's appreciation of Oriental art is also reflected in the substantial number of prints relating to landscape, *Radar Detecting Winter* (Ill. p. 45), *Radar Detecting Spring* (Ill. p. 48), and *Winter Tree* (Ill. p. 61) among them. The art of landscape is all but axiomatic to Canadian art; historically, it has been the dominant tradition of Canadian painting. The opposition of Painters Eleven to the Group of Seven and their successors is indivisible from the older artists' ideological appropriation of landscape as Canadian art. But the structure of abstract painting has been profoundly informed by responses to landscape. This is as evident in the work of Borduas and Jean-Paul Riopelle in Montreal, as it is in that of Macdonald, Mead, Nakamura, and Ronald in Toronto. Town's approach, even in the early works, depends less on the linear and mass structure of landscape – the horizon line articulated by vertical elements, the balance between earth and sky – than on landscape as the locus of myth and as a complex of forces: life and death, threat and repose, reassurance and destruction. His admiration of Tom Thomson (set down in the book he and David Silcox produced in 1977) arises from that sense of the power in landscape transformed by colour at the border of abstraction and representation.[7]

Winter Tree (Ill. p. 61) is less a description of natural form than the revealing of natural change. Coolness of colour, bareness of form, and a sense of decay predominate, but between these are memories of fall colours in the red strips, emerging as if in relief, and, buried deep in the heart of the print, an area of green within the greyness that hints at the revival to come. The sensitivity of the colour is matched by his choice of materials for printing, pieces of masonite and felt that relate to the firmness of the wood and the flexibility of leaves. *Radar Detecting Spring* (Ill. p. 48) is like the scan of a cathode ray that can pick up not only the surface colours but a presentiment of the future; through the earth brown and green ground and an area like a strip of unmelted snow, we see delicate greens and blues and reds, touches of gold and silver. *Seaburst* (Ill. p. 65), reminiscent of Hokusai's *Wave* woodblock print, is seen through a memory of Leonardo's *Deluge* drawings, oscillating the image between the narrative and the apocalyptic.

In important respects the closest parallel to Town's single autographic prints are the 1942 gouaches of Borduas. I am not suggesting any narrow tracing of influence, nor proposing common artistic aims, but rather pointing to the importance these works had for each artist's independent invention, for their intensely private investigation of form and imagery that set the course for future work.[8] Through these series of works both artists, at crucial points in their careers, stated positions independent from the advanced art around them – Borduas from the surrealism and cubism that Pellan's work had introduced in 1940 to Montreal with such an impact;[9] Town, from the drive for abstraction and its particular reference to New

Winter Tree
Single Autographic Print

York Abstract Expressionism. The sense of independence in the whole range and process of Town's prints is most particularly symbolized in *Departure of the Alphabet* (Ill. p. 63). The alphabet, the raw means of bringing form and expression to knowledge, has broken away from its sources, setting off uneasily on its journey.

The prints struck a course distinct from the art around him; by expanding the technique, Town opened an immense range of reference and meaning, and foreclosed the possibility of followers. He pressed the limits of a discipline, as if he were working *for* the difficulty imposed by restrictions rather than seeking solutions to pictorial 'problems.'

In today's changing climate in the visual arts – the swings of fashion and the seriousness of curatorship – the massive international juried shows and prizes have lost something of their prestige. In the 1950s, however, they were significant events, particularly for Canadian audiences which had been brought up on the hegemony of the art societies with their broad range of membership and their jury systems. Town's participation in these international shows was much more a measure of success then than it would be now. The rule of the marketplace was not then the popular benchmark of recognition.

From the time Braque glued that first piece of printed paper to a canvas in 1912, collage, montage, and assemblage became an integral part of twentieth-century art history. Each generation of artists has had to find its own way of using these techniques. Town has used and mixed all of them. His earlier works of the late 1950s are collage in being primarily, although not exclusively, paper products glued to masonite boards; his current works (Ill. pp. 194-199) are assemblages both because they are created from a variety of found objects and because their scale and format are determined as they are constructed.

His early collages were usually made on masonite, occasionally on plywood. Masonite, available in sheets eight feet by four feet, was relatively cheap and light. A few collages such as *In Air Above the Poet's House* (Ill. p. 77) were made on the full sheet; a few like *July* (Ill. p. 73) and *Garden for Eurasian Princess* (Ill. p. 37) used the full width of the sheet but less than the maximum height. Most often, however, he cut the sheets in half, producing two four-foot square planes.

In one of those nice and telling coincidences it was when Town was spending a substantial amount of his time on collages that Clement Greenberg wrote an article about collage. Isolating the importance of collage to the pictorial developments of Braque and Picasso in the years immediately before the First World War, Greenberg was generally dismissive of the technique in its subsequent manifestations. He found that collage was often used for mere shock value, and although "Arp, Schwitters, and Miró grasped its plastic meaning enough to make collages whose value transcends the piquant,...

Departure of the Alphabet 1957
Single Autographic Print

the genre otherwise declined into montage and stunts of illustration, or into decoration pure and simple."[10]

Whatever whim or ironic gesture prompted Braque's and Picasso's first experiments in collage, they revealed a way to invert traditional pictorial illusionism. Any means of artistic expression that gains the methodology of a technique can become a genre, no different from any other form or style that usage transforms into convention; but there can be no question, historically or conceptually, that collage and assemblage have been special means by which individual artists have stepped aside, either from their own previous work or from the expectations of the time, in order to investigate new avenues.

Among contemporary Canadian artists one can point to the collages Michael Snow made in the mid-1950s, the constructions of Gordon Rayner and Joyce Wieland in the early 1960s, the collages Toni Onley made in 1960-61 from pieces of paintings he had rejected, and Charles Gagnon's box constructions that seem to mark periods of reflective criticisms of his own work. Collage, as used by these artists (five among many), has questioned the assumptions of meaning in painting, questioned the relationships between making art and the fiction, the illusion, on which art depends.

Collage to Town's work has been fundamental, both as a technique and, in a broader sense, as a process of expression. While certain groups of his work obviously meet the technical definition of collage – gluing materials to a surface – his use of the underlying process of collage is pervasive. The structure of so many of his paintings bears directly on the process of collage.

Town began making collage-like works in paint in the early 1950s. One small group of pictures of 1953 to 1954 includes *Bagatelle* (Ill. p. 72), in which direct painting is combined with pieces of dried paint skins shaped and glued onto the masonite. They may have been made tongue-in-cheek, "mere trifles" as the title *Bagatelle* suggests. Nonetheless they have significant undertones, not only in the making of collage and its future importance in his work, but also as a critical comment on the "seriousness" of painting, and its weighty history of expressive illusion. Its history seemed all the more weighty at that time because of the prominence of Abstract Expressionism and the meaningfulness of the painterly gesture. In the end, painting itself is a bagatelle, no more than a skin of material.

The model for Town's range and extensive use of collage lies in the work of Kurt Schwitters – the meaning in the transformation (the *Entformung*) of banal materials into art through the individual essence (the *Eigengift*) innate in the materials. (Both German words contain curiously collaged linkings of positive and negative.) Central to Schwitters's collages and assemblages is the tension between the abstraction of art and the prior meanings carried by the materials used. That tension was held in the forming process, the metamorphosis of the materials by the structure of the collage. Schwitters "always responded to the stimulus of details

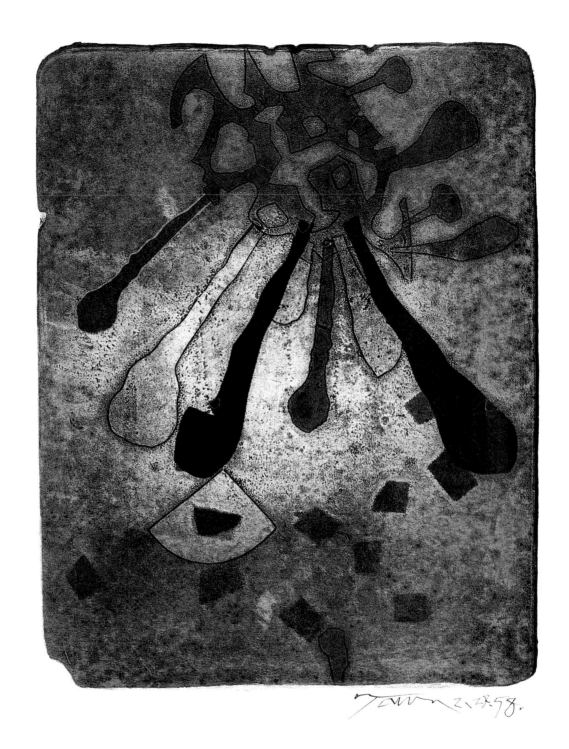

Seaburst 1958
Single Autographic Print

not formed by myself."[11] His was not a simple delight in a variety of materials, but a whimsical underlining of common sense, in that our perceptions of the world, both tactile and optical, depend upon our responses to stimuli not formed by ourselves. We cannot be apart from objects of perception. We draw in the scattered stimuli and order them by abstraction. Collage, as Schwitters used it, was to retain the tension (and the tragedy) between materials recognized as ripped from their context and the (impossible) attempt to deny them through their transformation into the abstraction of art.

But if Schwitters's collages are hermetic, Town's are open. In practical terms the distinction lies in the differences in scale, and in the contrast between the geometric construction of Schwitters's work and the freedom of structure in Town's collages. Schwitters's collages are invariably small objects set into formats that could be picked up and read like a book. The close viewing they demand is part of the irony of reading the details of materials, yet being held from narrative by the rigid abstract structure of the whole. They are sealed works, squeezing illusion into the tightest of planes. The collaged elements are invariably opaque and tend, in broad terms, to be similar in scale; emphasis lies on the chance attraction of a particular element, a word, an image, a splash of colour.

Town's collages, larger in scale – often much larger – include a wide variety of scales in the collaged elements, from small scraps of paper to quite large, clearly recognizable forms. He works with both opaque and transparent materials; he paints and draws through and around the collaged elements. The result is the opening to a wide range of viewing distances with a dynamic illusionistic impact dependent on the spectator's position. The overall impression gained at a distance is retained only as a memory as one moves closer and picks up details previously invisible in the larger view.

This sense of range in materials and the levels in the work varying with viewing distance must also be related to the time process in constructing the works. The early paintings were generally made in concentrated bursts of energy, often, as he has described, made under "violent impulse." The pace of the collages was quite different. He would work on up to forty at one time, gradually building up the surfaces, often having to search for exactly the right piece of material. Of *Garden of Nebuchadnezzar* (Ill. p. 67), for instance, he has said, "It took me over a couple of months to find the right piece of transparent paper for a section near the centre, on the right side. When I did find it, it was on a bottle of my wife's toilet water."[12]

There is no question that Town's concentration on collage in the later 1950s was a critical stance against the enthusiasm for Abstract Expressionism. The very character of his use and process of collage opposed the process of that approach to painting. But they also set, in crucial ways,

Garden of Nebuchadnezzar 1958
Collage and mixed media on masonite

Gateway to Atlantis No. 1 1957
Single Autographic Print

The Big Bite 1957
Single Autographic Print

characteristics that were to occur throughout his work even when he was concentrating on painting. Opacity and transparency, changes from distant to close-up viewing, interweaving drawing and planar forms, contrasts of textures, accumulation of heterogeneous elements, transformation of given shapes to the identity of the whole picture, the complexity of illusion, material flatness of the surface – all these characteristics essential to the collages find points of correspondence in the paintings of the 1960s and 1970s. For instance, the accumulated patterns of ringed shapes in the "doughnut" paintings are set against lines formed by masking out areas, as in *Optical* (Ill. p. 128) and *No-Op* (Ill. p. 131); they may also be used in reference to landscape, as in *The Great Divide* (Ill. p. 124). Similarly, from the contrasts of textures and materials, one can look to the curious juxtapositions of heavy impasto and large, flat areas of a single colour in the *Park* paintings (Ill. pp. 161-168). The imposition of fixed forms into the tension of illusion and flatness is taken up again in the *Tyranny of the Corner* paintings (Ill. p. 19 and pp. 106-107). Complexity in colour is also the basis of the *Snap* paintings (Ill. pp. 172-179) of the early 1970s.

In the variety of their textures, in the layering of painting and drawing with other materials, the collages develop a network of tensions that, held apart by the suggestions of illusion and association, open on to the play between the objects surrounding us and our memories and fantasies. It is a network that recalls the description by Robert Musil, the early twentieth-century Austrian writer, of adolescent awakening in *Young Törless*. Törless seeks to reconcile the mystery of how we perceive in imagination only indistinctly, as from a distance, but we act in the immediate physicality of the world. Between them is an "invisible frontier, and in it the narrow gateway where all that ever happens, the images of things, must throng together and shrink so that they can enter into a man..."[13]

Since his boyhood Town had been profoundly impressed by the collections of the Royal Ontario Museum. And the influence of the place was direct and decisive to his making collage. He saw the whole museum as a collage, he was struck by the essential interrelatedness of everything. "To me the Museum is like a miracle, like one of those Chinese boxes that open up, filled with miracles. Currelly created a toy for the whole city."[14] C.T. Currelly, a Mediterranean archeologist, was the first director of the Museum founded in 1912. Town dedicated *Monument to C.T. Currelly No. 1* 1957 (Ill. p. 75), one of the finest of the early collages, to Currelly for his work in building up the museum's collections. The collage is not simply a monument to collection, to accumulation; it is about the magic of transformation, whereby simple objects and fragments hold mystery and meaning for the imagination. In the centre of the collage is a single autographic print. Seen vertically it is a figural monument, like a box marked with or containing signs, equipped with a handle and string on the right that can open and close its lid. A mass of fragments falls down from above,

Odd Wheel Out 1958
Collage

Bagatelle 1954
Oil and collage on masonite

July 1957
Collage

scattered pieces from everywhere that, funnelled into the box, wait for anyone who will recognize their meaning. But the image may also be seen as if from above, looking down on the museum as a little island of miracles surrounded by darkness.

The *Monument to C.T. Currelly No. 1* is, in a number of ways, a key to so much in the collages. It was begun immediately after two others related in theme, *Square in Nineveh* and *Garden of Nebuchadnezzar* (Ill. p. 67). They gather in his fascination with the past, at this time in particular with Babylonian and Hittite cultures. (Nineveh was destroyed by the Babylonians and Medes shortly before Nebuchadnezzar became King of Babylon.) In *Square in Nineveh* and *Garden of Nebuchadnezzar* this fascination is manifested not by building a single, monumental image but by transforming the scattered fragments of the present, through the dynamics of imagination, into the layers of the past. He locates his fascination first in his personal interests and then, through the achievements of a man such as Currelly, to something of value established here in Toronto.

The challenge to current pictorial arguments cannot be separated from the art and events of distant times, nor from Town's living and working in Toronto. There is no escaping the tensions between the natural and urban environments, any more than the exchange between totemic images and toys, or the contrasts between extreme elegance and the grotty. And above all, there is the conviction that nothing must be wasted, for nothing is finally lost, whether in our experiences or opinions, through our perceptions or in the material that surrounds us.

It is an approach to collage quite different from that of Robert Motherwell, who has described collage as "both placing and ellipsis."[15] Motherwell's collages are built from a few discrete elements and a strictly limited buildup of one element on another. Town, even in a relatively simple formal structure such as *Architectural Trial* 1960-61 (Ill. p. 78), assembles and works with a complex of materials and techniques: a plywood crate, hydro-cal over hessian with burnt plastic containers, corrugated paper, fluorescent light packing, paint skin, pencil shavings, tissue paper, egg carton, silk stocking, wicker basket, golf ball, and metal bottle top. And paint. The emphasis lies, not as in Motherwell's collage, in lightly touching one finely chosen piece with another; rather the emphasis is on the holding of the whole work and on our recognition of the conflicts among the fragments wrenched out of their normal context. The interrelatedness of everything transcends disintegration.

This is presented from a totally different perspective in the *Death of Mondrian No. 1*, 1961 (Ill. p. 79). The structure of controlled illusion in Mondrian's paintings is inverted by arranging pieces of cardboard for the planar spaces and then burning their edges. This may seem merely the iconoclasm of the rebel, the challenge by the new to the enshrined; but the critical challenge is not so much a latter-day Dadaist gesture, as it is a

Monument to C.T. Currelly No. 1 1957
Collage

A Child's Christmas in Toronto 1961
Oil and lucite on canvas

In Air Above the Poet's House 1956
Collage

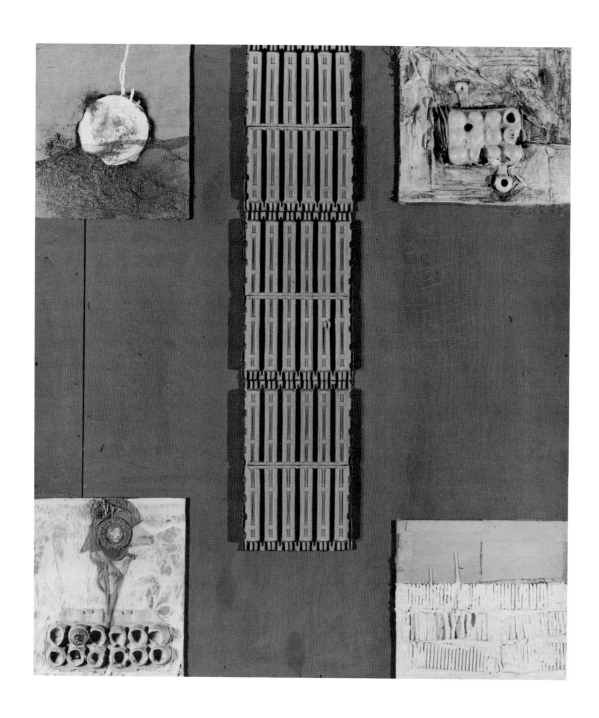

Architectural Trial 1960-61
Collage

Death of Mondrian No. 1 1961
Collage

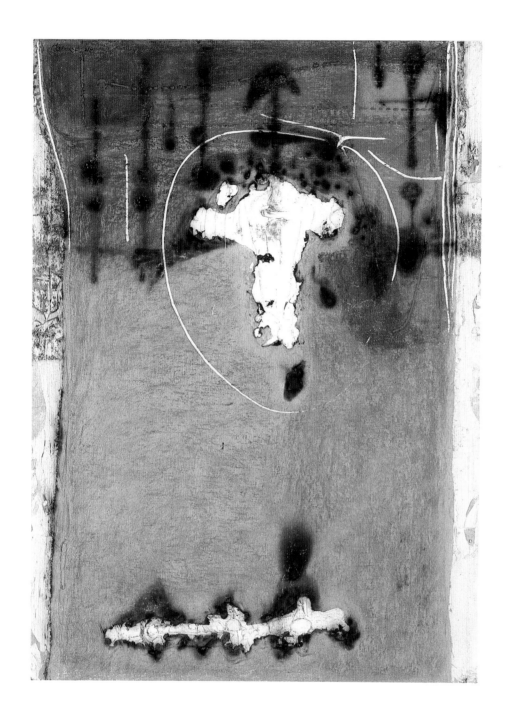

Epiphany 1960-61
Collage

The Abstract Expressionist Kid's Punch-Out
1960-61-62
Collage

questioning of shibboleths. It is a dispute with the orthodoxy that covers the work of Mondrian like a fungus, concealing the art. For art history tends to further the interests of interpretation rather than to consider the values and even the visibility of art. The work of Mondrian is not so much looked at as it is consumed.

Town holds open these issues by refusing the security of a line of development and by refusing what, in the avant-garde, was becoming the orthodoxy of dissent. Even within the collages there is a wide range of materials and approaches. They exist not merely for variety, but as the challenge of difference through which experience is confronted and questioned and opened beyond the surface. It is not enough to talk about collage as a genre, fixed in characteristics and expectations, for it must accommodate both the brilliant elegance of *Entrance of the Stage Left Dragon* (Ill. p. 15) and the tough and scrappy *Hokusai See-Through*, 1958-60 (Ill. p. 83). The first responds to a Japanese refinement, less perhaps of Japanese painting than of the embroidered patterns of ceremonial kimonos. The second is an ironic statement on that elegance. The principal drawing is done from the back, staining through the linen, as if we see only scraps of the real thing. Then the surface is burnt and the centre so weakened that a crushed egg carton almost pushes through it. The first embodies the elegance of an art arising from the sophistication of a culture; the second is a destructive angry response to a culture, our own, that stands, as it were, on the wrong side.

All of this is inseparable from his interest in and respect for distant cultures and his affection for and frustration with Toronto. "Ideas come from everywhere in the world to die in Toronto. We are a cultural compost heap, a rich metropolitan humus in which, if we can only control the expressway barbarians, greatness might just grow."[16]

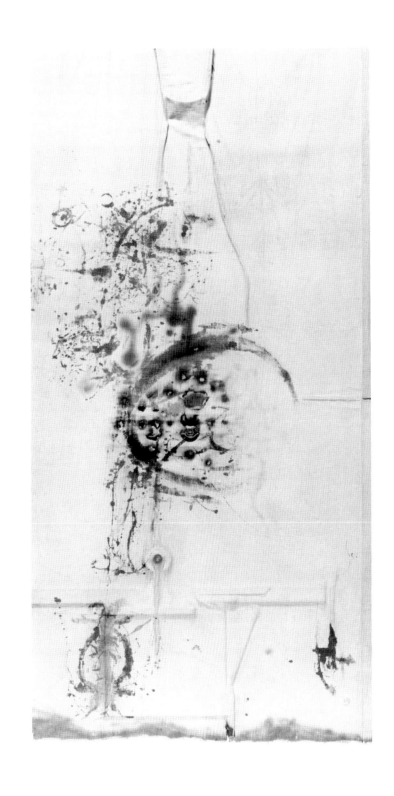

Hokusai See-Through 1958-60
Collage

FOUR

Controversy over Town's art began as early as 1951, when the painting *Two Nudes* was included in that year's Royal Canadian Academy exhibition at the Art Gallery of Toronto. Coming on the heels of the complaints raised when *Sailors and Floozies*, by the American realist Paul Cadmus, had been shown at the 1950 Canadian National Exhibition, Town's picture caught the full blast of moral outrage led by the newspaper *Flash* ("No Fear—No Favor—the people's paper"). "It's all there," the editor raged, "everything! Nothing is left to the imagination – nothing!"[1] Nothing, except that curious prurience in the self-proclaimed righteous.

Seven years later Town's work was again at the centre of controversy. This time, however, the event was one of those remarkable breakthroughs with results as incalculable as they are pervasive. On this occasion, Town was being commissioned to paint a large mural at the Robert Saunders Generating Station at Cornwall, one of the major engineering projects linked to the building of the St. Lawrence Seaway. Plans for the Seaway had been stalled in the United States' Congress although the project had the support of President Eisenhower. Through the initiative of the Canadian Government work was begun in 1954. Its realization sealed a major link, materially and symbolically, in Canada-US relations.

The commission to Town was remarkable for a number of reasons. The whole Seaway project was a massive undertaking, high in public interest and profile. It was, therefore, of special significance that Ontario Hydro which had responsibility for building the generating station, should commission a young painter – Town was then thirty-four – known for his links with abstract art (and hence, in the minds of some, with rabid irrationality). The recommendation had been made by Cleeve Horne, art consultant for the project. (This, in itself, was an important move as appointing an artist as consultant for public art commissions was still rare.)

The choice on the Canadian side was bolder still, as the commission for a mural at the corresponding plant on the American side fell to Thomas Hart Benton, one of the leading Regionalist painters, then in his late sixties, whose career had been devoted to American Scene realism. Benton's painting was a historical tableau depicting the meeting of Jacques Cartier and the Iroquois on the St. Lawrence. Town's painting was thirty-seven feet of extroverted energy in great sweeps of paint and broad, open forms.

Robert Fulford, praising both the work and Cleeve Horne's success in persuading Ontario Hydro to accept Town, wrote, "Their art should be just as advanced as their engineering."[2] Pearl McCarthy described the commission as a "proper use for abstraction," and underlined the contrast between the works on the American and Canadian sides by her disparaging reference to Benton's "pictures of Cartier and Indians."[3] There was, of course, opposition, but even Arthur Reaume's attempt to force the issue in debate at the Ontario Legislature made no headway. It was as if the euphoria raised by the success of the Seaway project had found its symbol.

The Dixon Passing Mugg's Island 1956
Oil on masonite

The public attention that was drawn to contemporary Canadian art by the Seaway commission reflected substantial changes in the Toronto art world. The traditional core centring on the Societies' annual exhibitions was eroding. The impact of the Painters Eleven had taken hold, and galleries with a commitment to showing advanced contemporary art were opening: in 1955 Avrom Isaacs' Greenwich Gallery and Barry Kernerman's Gallery of Contemporary Art; and Bud Feley's Park Gallery in 1957. Town held a one-man show of paintings at the Gallery of Contemporary Art in 1957. Although this gallery was only open for four years,[4] it had a significant impact on the emerging scene and showed, among others, Nakamura and Hodgson, Gershon Iskowitz, Louis de Niverville, and Robert Hedrick.

Important leadership also came from Alan Jarvis, Director of the National Gallery, who made a cross-country tour in 1955 specifically to buy works by contemporary Canadian artists. The same year the National Gallery held its first *Biennial of Canadian Art*, a series of exhibitions which continued through the 1960s. Although based on a jury selection, the exhibitions stood out from the hodgepodge that the RCA and OSA exhibitions had become, as they more closely followed the major international exhibitions that sought to identify the leading edge of art of the day.

For the first time there was a real sense of optimism, and for about seven years, from 1957 to 1964, there was something of a boom in the contemporary Canadian art market. This surge of interest followed by a couple of years a similar situation in the United States. It was led by some major collectors, Samuel Hirschhorn and Sam and Ayala Zacks in particular, but broadened by a substantial number of new collectors of contemporary art. The phenomenon was noted beyond the art review columns and art magazines: in 1961 Town was featured on the cover of *Maclean's*; inside, an article described "The Overnight Bull Market in Modern Painting."[5]

Town was to ride the crest of the wave. His reputation, which had been supported for ten years by a few writers, surged in a flood of publicity, unprecedented for a contemporary Canadian artist and unmatched since. His prolific output was channelled into a prodigious number of exhibitions. Between 1959 and 1964 he held fifteen solo exhibitions in Toronto, Montreal, Regina, Vancouver, New York, and Madison, New Jersey; in 1964, he was selected for the second time for the Venice Biennale.[6] During the same period he was included in almost seventy group exhibitions throughout Canada, and in Europe, Japan, the United States, and Mexico.

The most celebrated moment was the opening of his exhibition of paintings, collages, and prints at the Laing Galleries in February 1961. Thirty pictures were sold in the first two hours, within two weeks three-quarters of the extensive exhibition had been sold.[7] And the large oil paintings were as caught up in this frenzy of buying as were the smaller works on paper. It was an extraordinary situation, but for work that created an extraordinary excitement. Fulford wrote, "His real search is for

Enter the Empress 1960
Oil and lucite on canvas

Wright Flight (Memorial) 1961
Oil and lucite on canvas

Empty Burden 1961
Oil and lucite on canvas

the heroic gesture ... Down with timidity! Down with caution! Down with humility!"[8] And Pearl McCarthy used the show's success as an opportunity to condemn the small-mindedness that had marked the Toronto art scene since the 1920s: "We have been beset by artists, writers, sculptors, and architects of low ceilings who seem bent on cutting people down to size."[9]

These were heady moments. And not only for Town, although his exhibitions drew particular attention, his verbal barbs made excellent newspaper copy, and his own writing was widely published in newspapers and magazines. Younger artists, in particular, the "Isaacs Group,"[10] were gaining a share of the limelight. But the balloon began to deflate and in October 1964 the twenty-nine-year-old Gordon Rayner could be described, with fatuous irony, as "a sort of neglected grand old man of contemporary Canadian art."[11] The following year Harry Malcolmson wrote asking "Why Toronto has few young artists."[12] At the same time resentment against Town's extraordinarily high profile, *pace* Pearl McCarthy, began to come out into the open. Paul Duval wrote early in 1964 that "Today Town seems to seek the limelight for his every act" and weighed what he was gaining in publicity against what he "forfeited as a creative artist."[13]

But the matter went beyond personalities. The growth in collecting contemporary Canadian art had spurred curiosity and then knowledge about New York. If the growth of confidence, economically and culturally, had led to some premature notions of Toronto as the "New York of the North," the comparison, on closer examination, came up short. More contemporary American art was being shown in Toronto, particularly through the Jerrold Morris International Gallery which opened in 1962 (Town showed with Jerrold Morris between 1962 and 1969) and the David Mirvish Gallery, which opened in 1963. The development of modernism in Toronto had been described by its links with New York, but a question came to be asked in the mid-1960s: if New York, as it appeared, was being swept by the Pop Art phenomenon, where was the Toronto equivalent? The answer for some seemed to be that as Abstract Expressionism was abandoned by American and English artists for the newness of Pop Art, Toronto artists were reverting to the quintessentially Canadian subject – landscape.[14]

The confusion that knowledge of wider events seemed to bring led to tension and uncertainty, a polarization of opinion. On the one hand, Canadian art, judged within the context of the western art world, seemed to be moving back into provincialism; on the other, there was a growing sense of an exclusive cultural nationalism. Robert Fulford had written perceptively of this at the beginning of 1961. "Cancult," as he called it,

is not hard to spot but impossible to kill. It is a Cancult process by which literature and art are demoted to the status of a crutch for Canadian nationalism. It is a process which makes culture into an artificial historical event....

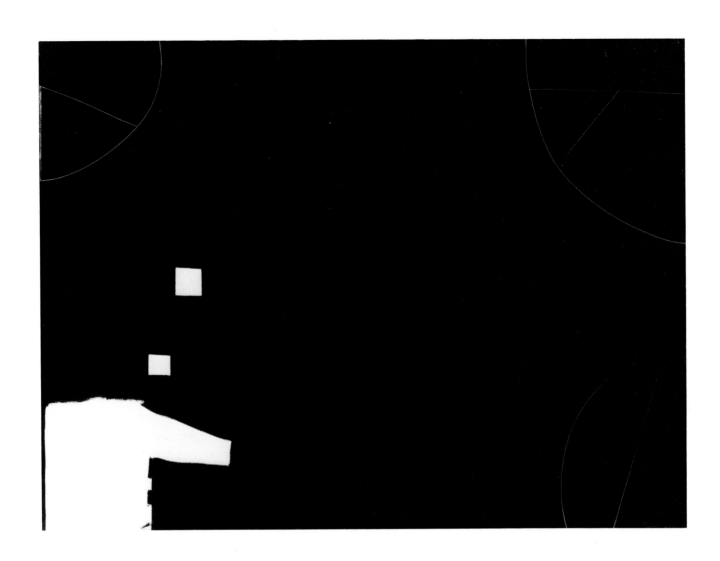

Cool One 1961
Oil and lucite on canvas

Great Seal No. 1 1961
Oil and lucite on canvas

He accused Cancult of being anti-cultural, Philistine, "because it holds that in a contest between art and nationalism, nationalism is more important," and gave as an example the way the Town's Seaway mural could be counted as "a part of our heritage before anyone notices that it is art."[15]

Town took a similar position in the "contest between art and nationalism" in the foreword to his book of *Enigma* drawings which was excerpted for a *Maclean's* article:

I wish to be part of a culture so sure of itself, that it makes the whole world of creativity come over the horns of our accomplishment, rather than silk-footed on the slither of a perennial red carpet…I love Canada, and am horrified by the fact that I feel compelled to say so."[16]

There was nothing proven by latter-day approximations of art elsewhere, any more than by protectionist self-assertion.

The still cool reality of the situation was symbolized by two events in 1965, as Barrie Hale has rightly pointed out.[17] In February the Women's Committee of the Art Gallery of Toronto organized a massive Happening, in which the public and artists got together in an art-making party. (Town and Yarwood directed the painting of a mural.) Four months later, in June, Dorothy Cameron was charged and subsequently convicted of showing "obscene objects" at her gallery in the *Eros 65* exhibition she organized. (That Town's drawings in the exhibition were not among those seized led to Kildaire Dobbs reporting the rumour that Town was "suffering from 'subpoena envy'."[18]) She was forced to close her gallery in October 1965. The fact is that the sense of "arrival" was premature. If the first event was "an apotheosis"[19] then in the minds of many it was a travesty and the wreaking of vengeance for such overweaning pride was not long in coming. Art in Toronto still existed on the margins of a society that had not yet become tolerant by indifference.

The sudden halt in what had seemed like an optimistic advance left Town still leading, but exposed. The extraordinary amount of attention he had gathered during that unusual moment made him a large target for critical sniper fire, particularly as he rarely declined the opportunity to return with both barrels. The "personality pieces" that had been written about him, the way that he was called upon and readily gave opinions and quotable copy were turned against him. He seemed vulnerable to the charge that so much talk and attention called into question the seriousness of the work. In 1964 Paul Duval criticized Town for remaining in Toronto and cutting himself off from the experience of great art:

I believe that Town's main flaw as an artist is not coldness but insecurity. His artificial take-offs on the styles of others I suspect originate from his refusal to believe that he has warm and unique things of his own to say about his world.[20]

Dennis Reid was more concise and dismissive of Town's historical place, when he described in 1973, the "'setting' of Town's brief sun-like presence on the Toronto scene [around 1965]."[21] And more recently Hale has described how

for a while [in the 1960s] no Toronto lawyer's, doctor's or dentist's office was without its Town drawing, smoke drawing, print or collage; no Rosedale or Forest Hill mantel without its Town painting, and this is apt enough, for the common currency of all these series is a copiously decorative, neo-baroque sensibility that mirrors the surface of the times;...[22]

And to ensure that Town cannot try to slip through by the "commitment to Canada" route, Barry Lord in 1974 slammed that particular door:

Town's refusal to pay Greenberg's fare [in 1957], like his moving into the Group of Seven's old Studio Building, and his comparisons of his colour and texture to those of Tom Thomson, are all just the saleable cultural-nationalist poses of an artist who is really a sell-out. He is today the darling of the Art Gallery of Ontario Women's Committee and all right-thinking Rosedale matrons.[23]

Town himself in fact had foreseen this downturn in 1963, "Success destroys your privacy..." he said. "Anyway, I think it's just about the time for me to become unpopular."[24] It was, however, at about this time that the reception for his work in New York was most positive – "The results are never less than exciting"; "This arresting exhibition should be included on your visiting list."[25] And *Time* reported:

A Canadian, Town, brushed his way to international fame without ever leaving his native Toronto, now surging with creative activity. In his new works a kind of visual civil war is waged on the canvas as white cuts colour, black fights for attention, space and shapes bounce around like so many boomerangs.[26]

He also received very positive responses in Chicago through his exhibitions with the Sears Vincent Price Gallery. In Canada, public attention also remained high, as the stream of new work was exhibited, and his own writing gained in popularity – he wrote a column almost every month for *Toronto Life* from the end of 1966 until early 1971. But serious critical attempts to deal with his work were few and far between. Against an artist who could out-write and out-argue any critic, silence was the harshest weapon.

The substantive issue, however, lies in what is achieved as art, not what is successful in Rosedale nor metaphors of rising and setting suns. The fact is – and the point must be underlined – that by the early 1960s, the character of Town's art had matured and resolved, both in relation to the art around him and because, through his work of the 1950s, he had determined the range of his concerns and the means by which they were to be achieved. Most telling, in view of the concerns at the time, was the clarity of the relationship of his art to Abstract Expressionism. As early as 1959, Duval, reviewing Town's exhibition of drawings at the Laing Galleries, had spoken of Town's reaction against the extremes of Abstract Expressionism.[27] But his drawings, more than mere reaction against extremes, must be considered with his paintings of that time. Their *structural* approach to formation is intensely personal; and their range in subject matter and in the pictorial variety finds equivalence in the paintings.

Just two examples from the 1959-60 period – *Bacchante Attacked by a Panther* (fig. p. 95 top) and *Queen Elizabeth I* (fig. p. 95 bottom) – will reveal that structural approach. The symbolism of the panther shifted from the medieval image of gentleness, attracting other animals by its sweet smell, to that of sexual aggression by the sixteenth century. By the nineteenth century the image shaded to an alluring danger, a confusion of love and lust, as in Swinburne's description of the animal:

And tracking ever slotwise the warm smell
Is snapped upon by the warm mouth and bleeds,
His head far down the hot sweet throat of her –
So tracks one love, whose breath is deadlier.[28]

In the drawing, that conflict of sensuous aggression and fear is concentrated in the heads of the panther and the bacchante. A swiftness of lines for the panther's leap and the flight of the woman – a swiftness of descriptive exclusion – is transformed into a concentration of lines and tones and textures at the point of attack.

The whole syntax of linear texture is changed in the *Queen Elizabeth*; her image of impenetrable presence is transposed into the armoured richness of her clothing. The fullness of the figure, described by thin lines and a light wash, lies behind a flat structure of brushed black ink. The links between Elizabeth the woman and Elizabeth the Queen are made with such brilliant touches as the way the heavy hooked sweep that establishes her right shoulder subtends the thinnest and lightest line in the whole drawing, the line that describes the movement across her neck and shoulders. The range of these two drawings – in technique and in the quality of linear texture – is inseparable from expression; the relationship between graphic emphasis and interpretation is inseparable from the subject.

The paintings of the early 1960s have a structural equivalence to the drawings. No means of using paint is excluded – thin and thick paint are set together, paint fills planes or defines lines, as for instance in *Banners*, 1960 (Ill. p. 101), *Interior Pitch Out*, 1960 (Ill. p. 104), or *Inoutscape*, 1960 (Ill. p. 109). Each painting is treated, as it were, as a separate campaign in all of its elements – forms, handling of paint textures and colours, the making of space.

The range within each painting draws out the full range and capacity

Bacchante attacked by a Panther 1959
Pen, brush and ink on paper

Queen Elizabeth I 1960
Brush, ink and watercolour on Arches paper

Variation on a Variation 1957
Oil and lucite on masonite

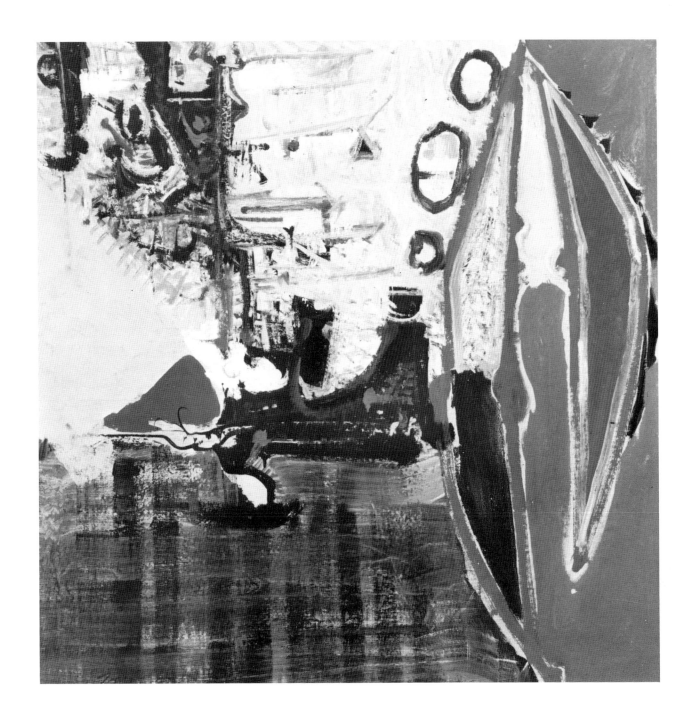

Landscape with Reed 1957
Oil and lucite on canvas

of the material itself, that is, oil paint. In a recent interview he described oil paint as "Harris tweed as opposed to the Dacron suit of acrylic" and as a material of intrinsic vitality: "…oils mirror life. Oils have a drying-dying time. You can use your oils in their youth, in their middle age, in their old age."[29]

This organic metaphor for the medium is equally apt for the way he creates the space of a picture. He does not use the area of the picture as a neutral, lightly resistant plane, but as a complete, vital form, in which each area must be differentiated, each part must realize its own character and yet not fail the whole. This was already apparent in the paintings of the mid and late 1950s, although at that time one can describe two somewhat different approaches that were later combined in the paintings of 1960.

Compare the 1956 *"The Dixon" Passing Muggs Island* (Ill. p. 85) and *Variation on a Variation* (Ill. p. 96) of the following year: the first comprises a series of locked forms, each differentiated in shape, colour, and painterly texture. The representational element – the ferry "Dixon" plying between Mugg's Island and the mainland – is abstracted and recombined in painterly equivalents that hold each part of the surface equally. *Variation on a Variation*, although it maintains some similarity in drawing to the earlier picture, centres a form within the space.

The link with the collages in these approaches to painting is both evident and necessary. And the same is true in his treatment of the sheet of paper in the drawings. For instance, in *Bacchante Attacked by a Panther*, the openness of the paper to the left shifts the illusion by a movement across the drawing to the conflict between the two heads, the girl's and the animal's. There all movement is stopped for a moment by the concentration of desire and rejection.

In *Interior Pitch Out* (Ill. p. 104) the looseness of the left side contrasts with the ordered flat plane on the right. In the centre, a frame-like body contains a ferment of painterly activity. This robot-like figure seems to be collecting a lump of form from the left, while presenting a second, neatly shaped by a black line, on a platter to the right. The painting seems to be a response to the very act of art making: raw material taken from nature is subjected to inner ferment, and then presented dispassionately as a finished object to a flat, bland world.

And if Town's efforts and his anger have ever been directed against any single characteristic, it is blandness: blandness in art, blandness in writing, blandness in people who avoid risks and resent those who take them. He has not failed to stand up for those who he felt were being wrongly attacked by the armies of the bland. When the architect John C. Parkin was under pressure, Town charged to his side:

He really is – and this is unforgivable in Canada – witty and urbane and cultured. If he were a boorish, bumbling, belly-button-pinching boob, then most of the third-raters who assail him would give him ten years of unmiti-gated eulogy.[30]

For Town has taken risks, in his art and in what he has said and written. And if his attacks have at times been unfair or misdirected, there has been no attempt to hide. His works and his personality have been out there in the public arena. His approach to his painting has been as his approach to everything. He has never been interested in incremental moves, in methodically building up a "development." Each painting or collage or drawing takes its own issue, not as part of a stylistic mean but as a particular pictorial moment, just as our perceptions and experience comprise a complex, diffuse and multi-layered individuality. It is curious that, at the peak of his public attention, when he was central to almost every discussion on art, his work was not only strikingly bold, but emphatically eccentric. But what is essential is that these characteristics in his art continued unchanged when the criticism of his work from the later 1960s became more voluble.

FIVE

The eccentricity of Town's work is based in the inventiveness of his imagery expressed by his rare control over painterly and graphic means and the independence he seeks for each picture. This means that even a small shift in emphasis from one picture to another can result in what appears to be a radical change in direction. This impression was all the more evident while painting was measured by the generalized assumptions, first of Abstract Expressionism and, subsequently, of post-painterly abstraction. The desire for orthodoxy that marks so much writing on modernist art history values the rationalization of disjuncture in appearance between the work of one generation and the next: it must *look* different but not *be* different. Novelty must obey a "development." What in Town's paintings of the early 1960s could appear as "delightfully eccentric," came to be thought of as fickle. Support for his work (which has never been absent) was too often expressed as a sort of nostalgia for past triumphs, for the prints and the collages, for example, and the security of always being able to talk about the brilliance and virtuosity of his drawing.

But Town is, above all, an artist of continuity and, perverse as it may seem in view of his prodigious output in all media, of economy. For the independence of position asserted in the 1950s has been the ground from which all changes have arisen; his economy lies in the fact that nothing is discarded and nothing is lost. The same economy is also manifested in the collection of material things, from primitive sculpture to a fire truck of the 1940s, from magazines decades old to obsolete computer parts. Part of a copy he made of Lorenzo de Medici and cast while at Western Technical School was used, forty-five years later, in the assemblage *Yesterday, Today and Tomorrow* (Ill. p. 202).

It is with this in mind that we must look at the sequence of his work in the 1960s and 1970s, beginning with the *Tyranny of the Corner* series (Ill. p. 19 and pp. 106-107) of 1962 and 1963 and the *Set* paintings (Ill. p. 19 and pp. 111-123) of the same date. He described the origin of the *Tyrannies* in 1962 this way:

Painting is still to a great extent dominated by a central image; corners in most cases are like uninvited guests at a party, uneasy, and unattended. In my series 'Tyranny of the Corner' I have invited the corners to come early to the party, and tried, if anything, to make all the elements of the painting that arrived late, a trifle uncomfortable.[1]

This statement seems to set out a very direct, painterly problem. The *Tyranny* paintings are generally larger than their immediate predecessors and painted to a flat rather than an impasted surface. Many are based on dark-light contrasts rather than complex and aggressive colour mixtures. Moreover they seem to turn away from the bold, heroic gesture to the solution of a technical abstract problem. But we have to account for the words "uneasy" and "unattended" and the sense of "making uncomfortable"; in

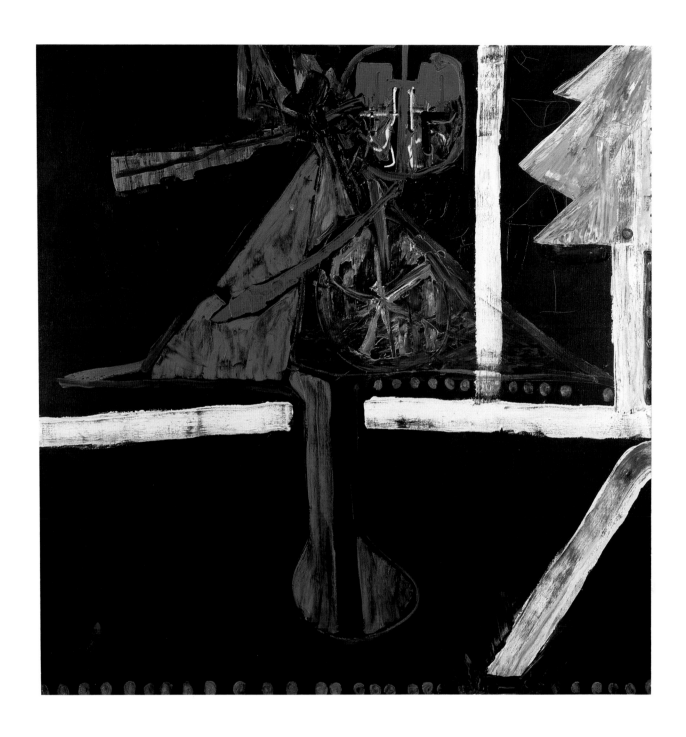

Banners 1960
Oil and lucite on canvas

short, we must question the willfulness of deliberately favouring the margins rather than the centre, and thereby jeopardizing the unity of the painting in both painterly and conceptual terms.

The issues raised by the *Tyrannies* were drawn from his earlier collages and paintings. This is most evident in the collage *Architectural Trial* (Ill. p. 78) with its solid anchoring at the corners. It is apparent, in a more subtle way, in *Odd Wheel Out* (Ill. p. 71). The wheel, not precisely circular, is set to one side. Its eccentricity is as though it has been displaced from its (rightful) position in the centre of the composition. In the boldness of holding open the centre, the collages went farther than the paintings of the same time. But the issue existed in them as well, both structurally and metaphorically. For instance, in *Banners* (Ill. p. 101) and *Interior Pitch Out* (Ill. p. 104) the pictorial space is divided into distinct areas of activity. In *Interior Pitch Out*, the dominant, centralizing form, which gathers all the colour and painterly activity, is a mediating element joining the space to the left with the space to the right. The same pictorial issue was developed, through quite different metaphors, in two other paintings of 1960, *Pitch Out* and *Juggling in Rousseau's Dark* (Ill. p. 103).

Pitch Out (Ill. p. 105) is a wonderfully funny picture, drawing on the central figure of a baseball team, the pitcher, and that tactical move of deliberately pitching wide to give the catcher a better opportunity to throw out a runner if he tries to steal a base. (If Jack Bush identified with the batter, wanting to "knock the ball out of the park,"[2] Town is the pitcher with a repertoire of curves, sinkers, sliders, and "change-ups" mixed with his fastballs). The pitcher in the centre of the diamond must be acutely aware of the runners at its corners, and the open spaces beyond to which the batter seeks to hit. When the focus is on the controlling figure at the centre, the corners are charged with danger for him.

Juggling in Rousseau's Dark, too, is built around a central diamond shape that seems to hover like a kite. The bright red circle passes through it like a ball being juggled between icicle blue hands; the kite and ball suspended in the air appear threatened by the encroachment of the corners. Structurally, the painting is very similar to *Pitch Out*, metaphorically it points playfully in quite another direction. It is, perhaps, an echo of the opening words of Rousseau's *The Social Contract* (1762) ("Man is born free; and everywhere he is in chains"), which describe the conflict between individual freedom and the bonding of the individual to the demands of society.[3] In these and other pictures of the time, Town critically confronts the questions of overall surface and image, animating the conceptual distinctions between them in painterly conflict, through shifting metaphors.

In the *Tyranny of the Corner* series he explicitly turns attention to that conflict by beginning with the corners, giving them prior place, and requiring the elements of the centre to adjust or to fight back. Compared to the paintings leading up to them, the *Tyrannies* are, in general, subdued in

Juggling in Rousseau's Dark 1960
Oil and lucite on canvas

Interior Pitch Out 1960
Oil and lucite on canvas

Pitch Out 1960
Oil and lucite on canvas

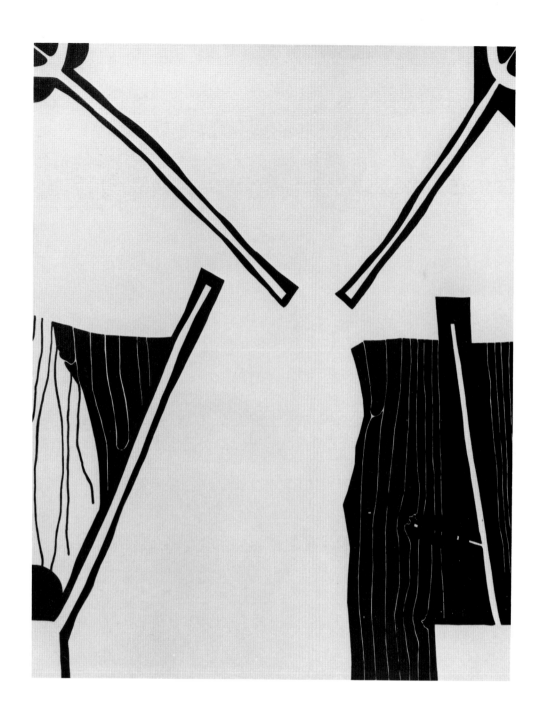

Tyranny of the Corner, Cliffhanger 1962
Oil and lucite on canvas

Entrance of the Tyranny of the Corner 1962
Oil and lucite on canvas

Festival 1961
Oil and lucite on canvas

Inoutscape 1960
Oil and lucite on Belgian linen

colour. A number of them, such as *Cliffhanger* (Ill. p. 106) and *Arabesque Set*, are restricted to black and white. In these he works not only with directionality across the picture plane, from the corners to the centre, but also with the sharp but shallow contrasts of negative and positive forms. *Cliffhanger* is a continual reversal of shapes and directions and illusion. There is no certainty, no outcome, like a cliffhanger of a film or a book, and the spectator is directed to an open centre that reflects only uncertainty.

In another group of the *Tyrannies*, for instance, *Card Set* 1962 (Ill. p. 115), he deliberately broke down the assumptions of directionality by first staining and dripping thin washes of paint across the surface and then turning the picture through ninety degrees to overpaint across the flow. The result here is not so much a clear dominance of the corners as it is the chaos caused in the centre, like the ruin of an evening.

In *Tyranny of the Corner* (Collection Canada Council) and *Entrance of the Tyranny of the Corner* (Ill. p. 107), the signs that mark the corners are emphatic. In a curious way, however, their assertion, defining the parameters of the picture, seem arbitrary, even uncouth, as they work against the delicacy of patterning and colour in the centre. The attraction of the corners, and the pressure they assert on the centre, strain and, in places, rip apart the cell-like structure of the painting, a structure that is reflective both of organic form and the weft and weave of the canvas.

In the course of the series the paintings become increasingly complex, more colourful, and more detailed. In *Tyranny of the Corner* (Ill. p. 116) (Collection Imperial Life) the tyrannical aspect of the corners appears compromised. Emphasis in the lower right is eliminated and the other three corners are reduced to decorative signs with limited influence on the centre.

In *Tyranny of the Corner (Traffic Set)*, 1962-63 (Ill. p. 117) the priority of the corners, their right of way, as it were, has been lessened. The arrow signs of some of the earlier pictures have been co-opted by the centre and have taken up positions as directional signs, ambiguously pointing both ways. There is an ironic confluence of road patterns and traffic signs and the totemic forms that Town developed in the single autographic prints. Those forms, which pointed into the core of the past, have been transformed into modern totems, the tyrannical signs of a present ruled by the automobile. People or pedestrians have been reduced to pathetic mushroom-like forms that are pushed, ordered, and threatened by the authority of the road. An ominous dribble of red paint courses down the picture; any discomfort at the centre is that of the herded pedestrians. The tension in the earlier paintings that questioned the hegemony of the centre has been inverted, just as the rules we create for civil order are turned back on us as authoritative imperatives.

The *Set* paintings (the reference of the series is to stage sets) are related in a number of respects to the *Tyrannies*, and some paintings carry both

Uncas Set No. 2 1962
Oil and lucite on canvas

For Corbu 1960
Oil and lucite on canvas

Armoured Explorer 1961
Oil and lucite on canvas

Pursuit Set 1962
Oil and lucite on canvas

Card Set 1962
Oil and lucite on canvas

Tyranny of the Corner 1963
Oil and lucite on canvas

Traffic Set 1963
Oil and lucite on canvas

terms in their titles. *Copernicus Set* (Ill. p. 120) layers metaphor on metaphor; any emphasis put on the corners to stress the picture plane serves equally as the means for its dissolution. The central form is like a map of the night sky, and the disposition of the stars has the order of an astronomical table. Our understanding, however, remains confined; the range of our horizon limits what we can see. Just as the difference between the pre-Copernican and Copernican systems is that of a fixed and a relative concept of the heavens, so the totality of our vision is loosened from fixed boundaries. Shapes repeat themselves, but their location shifts from secure anchorings to forms that seem to be floating beyond the field of our perception.

The issues Town raised by the *Tyranny of the Corner* series are in part retrospective and in part a critical reaction to what was rapidly developing in the mainstream of painting during the early 1960s. It was retrospective in setting back the challenge of the central image, the totemic image, and reforming spatial illusion. The tensions in the *Tyrannies* were presented both in the switching between negative and positive spaces and in the pull or imposition of the corners on the centre. The "push and pull" – the central structure of abstract painting's illusionism – had also to be reconciled with the tensions across the surface.

It was at this time, in American art, that a cool simplification rose against Abstract Expressionism's late excesses. It was a simplification that coalesced shape, pictorial structure, and image, and all but isolated them from any identification beyond their own autonomy. At that time, the paintings of Frank Stella and Kenneth Noland were beginning to receive the major attention that would be heralded as a further stage to modernism's progress. It is now evident that the situation was a more complex one, involving the simultaneous emergence of Pop Art and Happenings, minimal sculptures and paintings.[4] In Stella's *Black Paintings* of 1959-60 the repetition of shape broke the tradition of figure-ground tension by all but equalizing the whole surface. His retention of the centre as the emanating point was ironic because the banality of the pattern ensured that the centre had only contingent significance. Noland, in his target and then his chevron paintings, also destroyed the hegemony of the centre, first by a head-on attack and then by displacing it by shape and colour. The myth of the centre was fully displaced in the artists' shaped canvases.

Town's approach in the *Tyrannies* was quite different in two important regards. He insisted, first, on the active, charged field of the painting, and second, on the related internal metaphoric character expressed in the structure of the painting. It is conservative, not in the sense of beginning with a (central) text or story, but in conserving the activity of artmaking as a particular and specialized example of expression. It is a view of art that became increasingly unfashionable through the 1960s. Ernst Gombrich projected that unfashionable view in a 1961 *Saturday Evening Post* article, "How to read a painting."[5] Gombrich opposed any deterministic approach

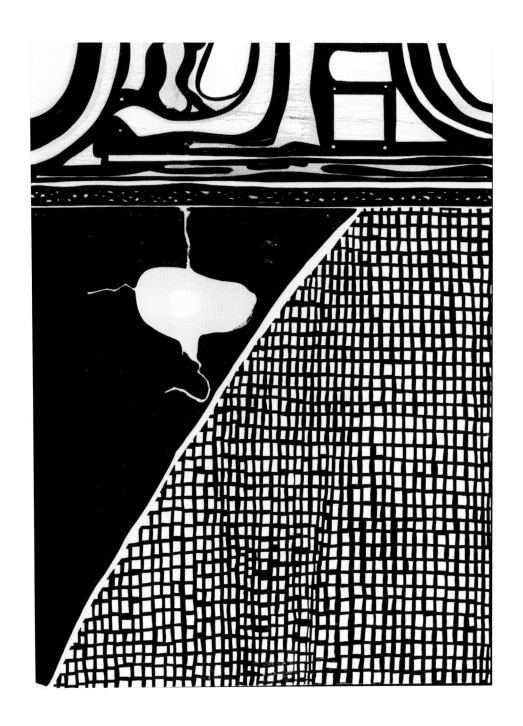

Parkin Set 1962
Oil and lucite on canvas

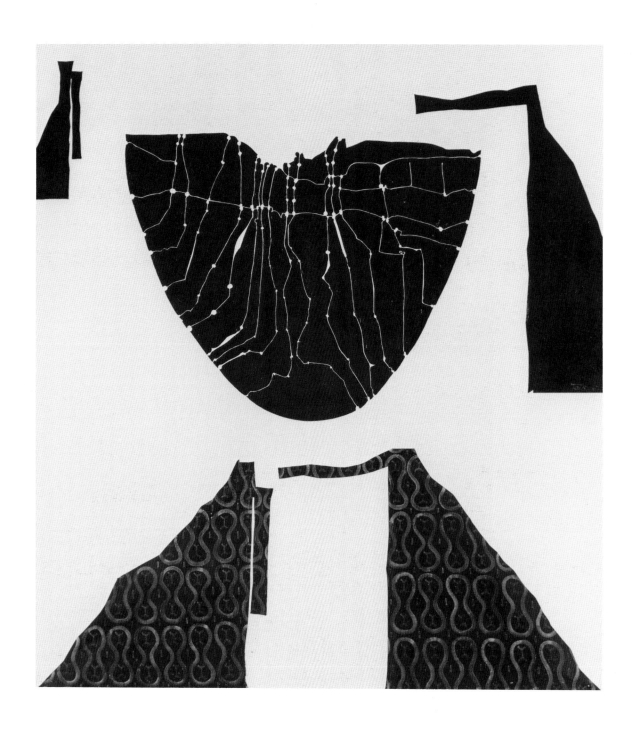

Copernicus Set 1962
Oil and lucite on canvas

Parade Set 1963
Oil and lucite on canvas

to picture making, and asserted the continuing value in the complexity of illusionism in reading a picture. He argued it was an oversimplification to claim that an image is absorbed as a whole rather than being perceived as an accumulation of parts.

The *Tyrannies* and *Set* paintings of 1962 and 1963 reasserted in a new form the purpose of Town's art that he had laid down in the 1950s. In them he reasserted his refusal to foreclose on painting's openness and potential for meaning first by dissolving and then by reclaiming the continuity of painting's irresolvable conflict between two and three dimensions. This refusal is critically stated in a very funny painting of 1961, *Armoured Explorer* (Ill. p. 113). An intrepid knight, a Don Quixote, in his full armour with lance held aloft, surveys the landscape of post-painterly abstraction. Town challenges the sententiousness of the style by the incongruous intrusion of the explorer into the "ambitious" scale of the painting. The "handmade" struggle for abstract form is being surveyed by a figure more cunningly drawn than anything he can see around him.

Town showed his new paintings at the Jerrold Morris International Gallery in April 1962. The press reports were still accounting for the phenomenon of the 1961 Laing exhibition: "[A Town exhibition] is to the world of Canadian art what the Grey Cup game or the Stanley Cup playoffs are to Canadian sport."[6] And then, for four years, he stopped showing his new paintings in Canada.[7] He did show outside the country, however, with exhibitions at two New York galleries, at Farleigh Dickinson University, and the New Jersey Museum. When he did show new paintings again in Toronto it was done with typical flamboyance. Exhibitions at the Mazelow Gallery and the Jerrold Morris International Gallery opened on the same day in January 1966 with Town being whisked between Bloor Street and the city limits.

These two exhibitions introduced an extraordinary group of paintings made in 1964 and 1965. Bold in design and brilliant in colour, they include some of the most striking paintings Town has ever done, such as *In Memory of Pearl McCarthy* (Ill. p. 125), *The Great Divide* (Ill. p. 124), and *Centrebiz* (Ill. p. 129). They were based on a particular graphic unit – what he has called the "doughnut" – and the technical device of using masking tape to create both negative and positive forms. The contrast between the "doughnuts" and the linear forms is, itself, a pictorial metaphor. Each of the "doughnuts" was painted freehand, each differs slightly in shape and colour and texture; whereas the linear forms were "mechanically" produced by painting in the areas defined by the tape. The density of detail and the powerful impact of the overall design completed the re-evaluation of pictorial space that he had undertaken in the *Tyrannies* but took even further the tensions in the movement between surface and depth, and opened the range of optical response from distant viewing to density of detail.

The cell-like structure of *Entrance of the Tyranny of the Corner* and

Sunday Painter's Set 1962
Oil and lucite on canvas

The Great Divide 1965
Oil and lucite on canvas

In Memory of Pearl McCarthy 1964
Oil and lucite on canvas

the doughnut-field of *Tyranny of the Corner* (Collection Canada Council Art Bank), 1962, with its black ground setting off the glowing golds and reds of the doughnuts, depended on the compression of detail set in tension by the pull and pressure of the corners. In contrast to these dense surfaces, in which every part exerted or resisted pressure, there is the curiously exploded *Helicopter*, 1963 (Ill. p. 127). Its strong, clear shapes are scattered over the white ground; a springing point, in the joining of the four black shapes, is set far to the top of the picture. It is as if, having been displaced from its rightful place in the centre, the form spins itself to destruction.

This contrast between the tight tension of the *Tyrannies* and the scattering of forms in *Helicopter* are brought together in the 1964 painting, *In Memory of Pearl McCarthy* (Ill. p. 125). The painting honours the longtime art writer for *The Globe and Mail*. McCarthy had been the first writer to give attention to Town's work; in 1944 she commented positively on his work shown in a student exhibition at the Ontario College of Art, and in reviewing the 1948 *Mayfair Artists Show*, she picked out Town's *Woman with Cat* for special mention. "Harold Town," she wrote then, "seems to have independence enough to resist the influence of famous moderns and try to get his own answers to the problems of form."[8] She died on March 25, 1964.

Both in its form and its meaning *In Memory of Pearl McCarthy* is like the engraved brass plaques on medieval tombs, monuments to the corruption of the flesh and the endurance of the spirit. This duality lies in the essential contrast between negative and positive shapes and between firmness and disintegration. It is as though we are looking down on the figure; we see in part a skeletal form, the shape of ribs, and a scattering of forms of a cellular breakdown. But, on the right, are three firmly defined forms, like a head with speech balloons emerging from it. And within these forms there are the characteristic "doughnuts," each individual, but clearly described and keeping perfect order.

The same elements of pictorial structure – the masking tape edges, the doughnut shapes, and the view from above – are given wholly different purpose in *The Great Divide*. Harry Malcolmson described the picture in his essay for the catalogue of the dual shows of 1966:

…a crackling sliver of white that could relate to a stream cutting through a landscape, looked at from the air. Doughnut shapes are brilliantly employed to suggest the even texture and subtle roll of the glaciated Northern Canadian hill. The entire canvas is suffused with the unshadowed golden light that floods the Northern landscape prior to sunset.[9]

The notion of the "doughnuts" as trees seen from above is even more powerfully made if we see the bared strips on either side as the slices made into a hillside by tree-felling.

Helicopter 1963
Oil and lucite on canvas

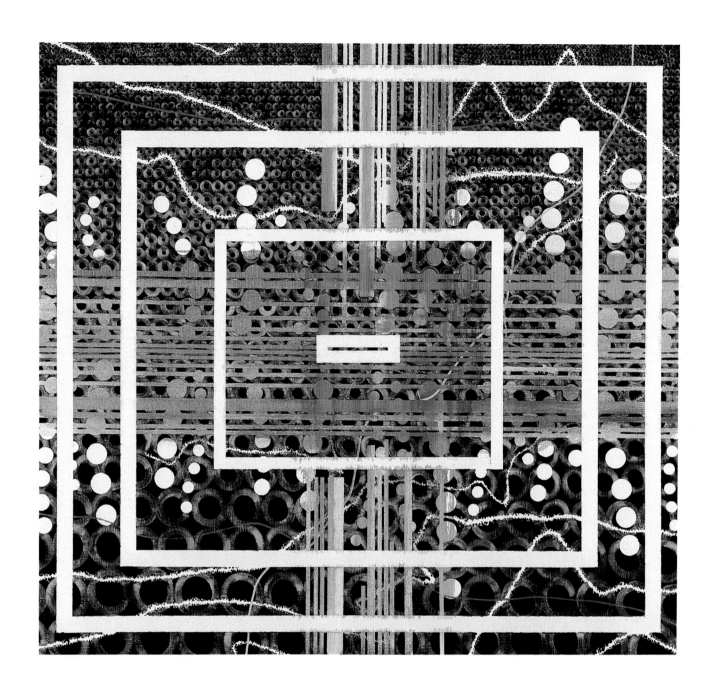

Optical 1964
Oil and lucite on canvas

Centrebiz 1965
Oil and lucite on canvas

Glory Hole 1965
Oil and lucite on canvas

No-Op No. 3 1964
Oil and lucite on canvas

The 1961 exhibition at Laing's had been a milestone, not only in Town's career, but in drawing attention to the vigour of contemporary Canadian art. The double exhibition of 1966 confirmed Town's preeminence, but it was a confirmation that separated him from the broadening range of concerns that were developing in Toronto. His rejections, by word and deed, of the growing influence of Clement Greenberg on both artists and writers, were themselves rejected as tiresome. Moreover, in one of those curious reverses in expectation, he seemed to be accused of failing to lead. It was as if the strength of his position in previous years somehow carried a responsibility for the collective health of art in Canada. It was a debt that he would not recognize and, in turn, his work from the mid-1960s were charged with extravagance and indulgence in "optical gymnastics."

Taken together, the works in the 1966 exhibitions show no more and no less than what had arisen from his previous work. Their premises of subject matter, painterly structure, and forcefulness were extensions of the bases of his painting. *In Memory of Pearl McCarthy* and *The Great Divide* asserted personal concerns – the recognition of people whom he respected and the importance of landscape as a constant point of reference. The sheer dazzle of pictures such as *Festival* (Ill. p. 108), *Centrebiz* (Ill. p. 129), and *Glory Hole* (Ill. p. 130) was a gesture of challenge, the challenge to push a painting against the grain of what should work, the challenge to timidity.

In *Optical* (Ill. p. 128), for instance, he sets up layer on layer of conflict: the doughnut shapes expand from bottom to top, the masked-out rectangles hold the surface and yet penetrate in depth, the vertical and horizontal bands of colour modify the colours beneath them but cannot contain the loose, script-like drawing. But with all this activity there is never, as Malcolmson pointed out, a violation of "the sanctity of the picture space enclosed by the sides of his canvas."[10]

The concentrated work on the "doughnut" paintings was followed by individual pieces that develop the optical effects of those works. *Dot*, 1966 (Ill. p. 134) is a loner, playing conceptually and visually on the weaving patterns of the eye across the surface. Against the illusion of pictorial structure directing the eye, *Dot* complies with the part by part accumulation of information and still confounds it by the desire to find a rational structure.

It is much more difficult to find the vitality of that tension in a piece like *Fate Curtain* (Ill. p. 133). For all the conflict between the optical texture of the "doughnuts" and the curving linear elements, the image of the whole stamps itself more strongly into stasis. Nevertheless, as we shall see, the painting is important as a bridge from the earlier "doughnuts" to the major series of the *Snap* paintings (Ill. pp. 172-179) of a few years later.

The principal series of paintings from the late 1960s and the very early 1970s were the *Stretches* and *Silent Lights*. Both series arose in response to particular situations.

Fate Curtain 1966
Oil and lucite on canvas

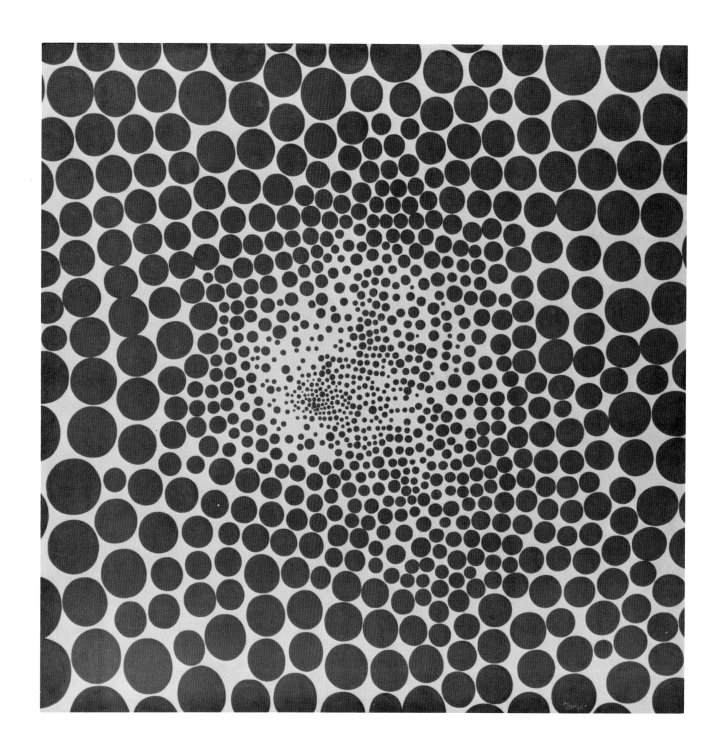

Dot 1966
Oil and lucite on canvas

Town worked on the *Silent Light* (Ill. p. 136) series between 1968 and 1970, each picture consumed many hours of work over months and, in some cases, years. The decoration of the Town Christmas tree has long been one of the great family events, an exercise massive in organization and execution. One year, the tree was so overladen with decorations that it toppled over, and the shards of smashed ornaments flew around the room. This disaster was redeemed when, collecting the shattered coloured glass, Town became fascinated by the sparkle and mixing of coloured light and he made a collage from the fragments. The *Silent Lights* (referring to both the Christmas carol and the disaster, which was by no means silent) explore this complexity of coloured light in ingeniously complex paintings, in which layer on layer of paint is laid down by progressive shielding with masking tape.

The *Stretches* of 1970-71 are, at one level, an homage to Matisse, in particular to the elegance of form in the late cut-outs. Against the complexity of the "doughnuts" and *Silent Lights*, the *Stretches* depend on a single simple form, such as a drop of paint drawn into a long stream, like a raindrop on a window pane. Referring to *Stretch 27* (Ill. p. 139), Town described how, "Everything stretches in our society; this picture is about pulling cellophane out of a box, or spilling ketchup."[11] At another level they are, in their simplicity of form and reduction of colours, a critical deflating of the high seriousness that was gathering in the later 1960s about "literal and depicted space," "ineluctable flatness," and other chimeras of formalist criticism. If what is wanted is flatness and the tension between picture shape, formal depiction, and coloured space, Town delivers all of them without giving up either humour or the values of drawing.

Still, for all their invention, for all their continuity with his previous work, and for all their ingenuity and their criticism, the *Stretches* and *Silent Lights* do not sustain the depth of the earlier series, nor of the *Parks* and *Snaps* that followed. They appear trapped rather than transformed by their virtuosity, and if they were received with little enthusiasm when shown in the early 1970s, they are not paintings that the perspective of fifteen years values in the light of subsequent development.

Those who claim a decline in the attack of Town's work, can most readily point to these series. However, these critics have wrongly overlooked the subsequent series of paintings, have been too ready to see them as mere continuations of a pattern. This, however, is a serious mistake, particularly with regard to the *Parks* and *Snaps* series. Both relate to the essence of Town's art and demand much closer consideration than they have hitherto received.

Silent Light No. 11 1968-69
Oil and lucite on canvas

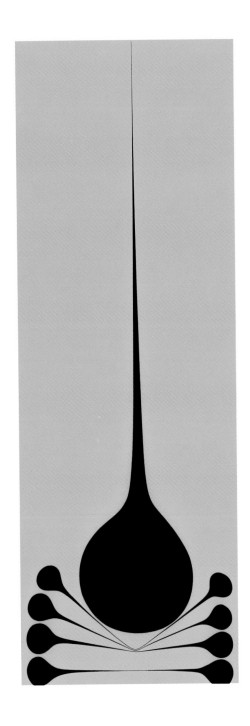

Stretch No. 23 1970
Oil and lucite on canvas

Stretch No. 30 1970
Oil and lucite on canvas

Stretch No. 27 1970
Oil and lucite on canvas

Stretch No. 3 1968
Oil and lucite on canvas

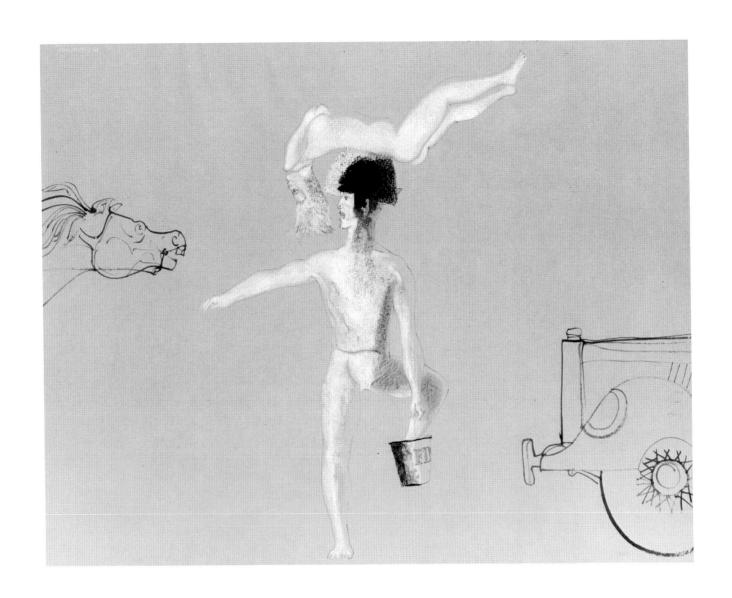

Enigma 1 1964
Brush, steel pen, black and white ink on
grey-green Fabriano paper

SIX

There is a sense – and it strikes me only because of the previous and later works – in which the paintings of the later 1960s had become curiously specialized. The density of the earlier paintings, their charged flow between pictorial invention and adventure and imaginative metaphor, seemed to be reduced. Yet this same period was particularly rich in drawings. The three series – *Enigmas*, the *Lady in the Cook Photos*, and the *Silent Stars, Sound Stars, Film Stars*[1] – are wholly distinct in approach, meaning, and appearance.

The *Enigmas* (Ill. p. 17 and pp. 141-152) were made during an eight-year period. An extraordinary series of satirical drawings, they range over a wide spectrum of contemporary life and issues, but they are unified in style, technique, and format – black and white inks in brush and steel pen on green or brown or grey papers that are similar in size. They are, as Town has said, "the political cartoons on my private editorial page." The *Lady in the Cook Photo* series (Ill. pp. 153-160) is an almost complete contrast. Completed over a relatively brief period between 1969 and 1971, their theme is taken from a nineteenth-century glass print photograph of a tightly corsetted, buxom woman. The image was made by a photographer named Cook, who had studios on Yonge Street. This image became the basis for a large series in a wide range of techniques and sizes, from nine by five inches to five feet high and three and a half feet wide.

The *Enigmas* were begun in January 1964. At that time Town was making the screen that had been commissioned for Toronto's Malton Airport. It was a slow process – etching in a mechanical acid bath set up in his basement –and while waiting for the acid to bite he would go upstairs and draw. In the course of a drawing he realized that the figure he was making was one he had done before. In frustration, hating to repeat himself, he put the foot of the figure in a bucket and suddenly the idea clicked; he transposed his own reaction to the drawing on to subjects and attitudes that frustrated him.

The series that began with that drawing, *Enigma 1* (Ill. p. 141), developed quickly. In the early months of that year he made a group of drawings in similar technique with subject matter that became immediately pointed, "With love I draw what I hate."[2] The series gained instant notoriety when ten of the drawings were included in the representation of his work for the 1964 Venice Biennale. Two of the drawings were found to be offensive by a cardinal, whom the *Chicago Tribune* nicely described as "a wandering prelate," who ordered them removed. This action played precisely into Town's hands:

It's such an honour being banned in Italy, the mother of sensuality. It's like being asked to straighten your tie in a bordello.... It's ironic that the pictures were removed on the complaint of a cardinal. I regard censorship as a cardinal sin."[3]

Enigma 1964
Brush, steel pen, black and white inks on
grey paper

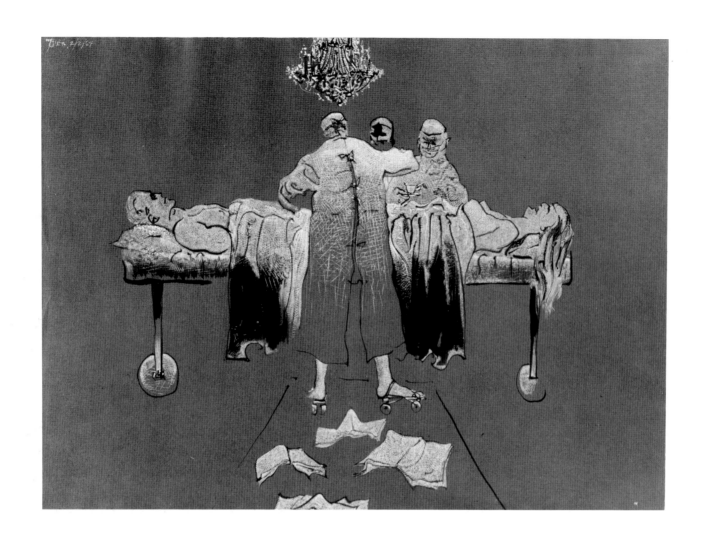

Enigma No. 9 1964
Brush, steel pen, black and white inks on
grey paper

Enigma 42 1966
Brush, steel pen, black and white inks on grey
charcoal paper

Town's drawings are a personal litany of dislikes and anger, of "specific private loathings" – of social wrongs and follies, of the hypocrisies, complacency, and self-seeking of those who hide behind the mystique of professionalism or the cosseted power of institutions.[4] He has said that the meaning of many of the drawings escapes him, referring more to the intuitive emergence of particular figures than to the obscurity of their themes. So many of the drawings have a nightmarish quality, flashes of sudden clarity against shadowy presences, a violent clamour that breaks through the surface of rational behaviour and expectations. Unlike the social criticism of Thomas Rowlandson or the satirical caricatures of clergy and princes by Annibale Carracci, Town's *Enigmas* most closely resemble the satires of Goya. Both use the characteristics of individuals but deny them anything more than a collective existence, which, when stripped of its veneer of civilization, reveals a pathology of psychosis.

In some drawings the satire is direct, as in *Enigma No. 9* (Ill. p. 144) which attacks the venality of the medical profession. A surgeon on roller skates, operating beneath a chandelier, appears to be joining a man and woman at the genitals. His indifference to the consequences of his work is surpassed only by his haste to get from one well-paying operation to the next. Other drawings relate to particular political events: *Enigma 1972* (Ill. p.152), for instance, satirizes the boost that was given to the Quebec separatist movement by President de Gaulle's meddling "Vivre le Québec libre" from the balcony of Montreal's Hotel de Ville on July 24, 1967.

Town has never made any secret of his opposition to the Canada Council's granting of government largesse to artists. *Enigma 2-4-17-4/66* (Ill. p. 145) strikes at the insidious implications for art when government is its primary patron. A motley and ragged crowd of artists clamour to bring their pathetic wares to the attention of a Louis XIV, idly holding out his foot to be kissed, deciding on whim to whom he should grant his favours. Beneath the elaborate throne, Town has contemptuously set the royal chamber pot, appropriately labelled.

Enigma 38, 1965 (Ill. p. 147) appears to take up the matter of the censorship of his drawings at Venice. A cardinal, seated on a modern office chair, glares lasciviously at a painting of sexual assault. The cardinal's hypocrisy is emphasized by the transformation of an amputation into a vicious but incapable hook-ended penis. Attended by a sister of the church and a militaristic fool holding a swastika emblazoned balloon above his master's head, the cardinal has momentarily turned his attention from the delights of the bottle, while to one side, an artist and a critic spout toadyish explanations.

The extraordinary power of the drawings lies in the tension between the harshness of the images and the range of linear textures and unbounded variety of detail. In *Enigma 38*, for instance, the fully drawn details of the cardinal's head contrasts with the empty caricature of the general;

Enigma 38 1965
Brush, steel pen, black and white inks on
grey-green paper

and both are set against a marvellous description of a dog drawn in a
scribble of black line. There is, too, the choice of the dull coloured
papers and the elimination of background detail, throwing all the emphasis onto the figures and yet condemning them to a world in which there
are no footholds.

Everything that gives meaning, both in subject and graphic means, in
the *Enigmas* is inverted in the *Lady in the Cook Photo* series. The *Enigmas'*
black humour and obsessive detail, the figures made from pen lines stab-
bing like the pins of a voodoo doll, are a world apart from the variations
on the well-rounded forms of that rather plain, anonymous figure in Cook's
photograph. Town approaches the subject with no preconditions or restrictions in style or technique, as if releasing all that bound flesh from the

147

Enigma 1967-68
Brush, steel pen, black and white inks cork
print on brown paper

Enigma 1967
Brush, steel pen, black and white inks on
brown paper

Enigma 1968
Brush, steel pen, black and white inks on
brown paper

Enigma 1972
Brush, steel pen, black and white inks on
green paper

restraints of her stays and the rigid formality of the photograph. Each
work in the series used a different technique and produced a different
image; from pen and ink on various coloured papers, to graphite and eraser,
to scorching the paper, to outlining the figure in glue in a sandwich of
illustration boards and then ripping them apart, even to a work made
from the impressions of a dressmaker's tracing wheel.

Both the *Lady in the Cook Photo* and the *Silent Stars, Sound Stars,
Film Stars* are based on photographs. The distinction Town makes between
them parallels the distinction Roland Barthes, in his study of photography,
makes between what he calls the *studium* and the *punctum*;

The studium *is that very wide field of unconcerned desire, of various
interest, of inconsequential taste.... Very often the* punctum *is a "detail,"
i.e., a partial object...However lightning-like it may be, the* punctum
has, more or less potentially, a power of expansion.[5]

Enigma 1972
Brush, steel pen, black and white inks on
brown paper

Lady in the Cook Photo 1970
Dry brush and ink on Mongolfier paper

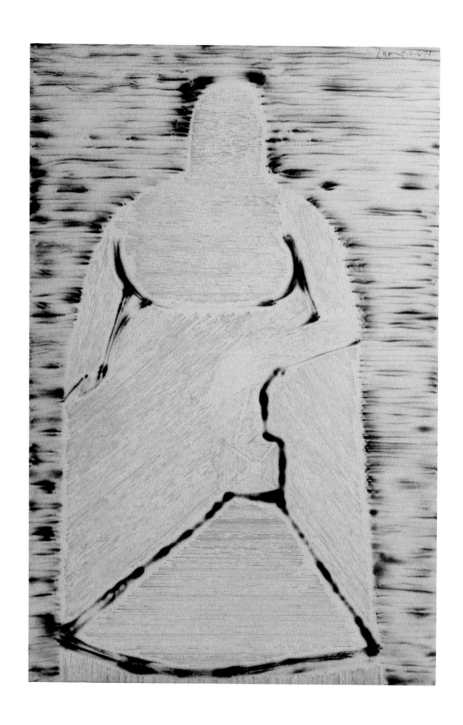

Lady in the Cook Photo 1971
Pen and ink, propane torch on crescent board

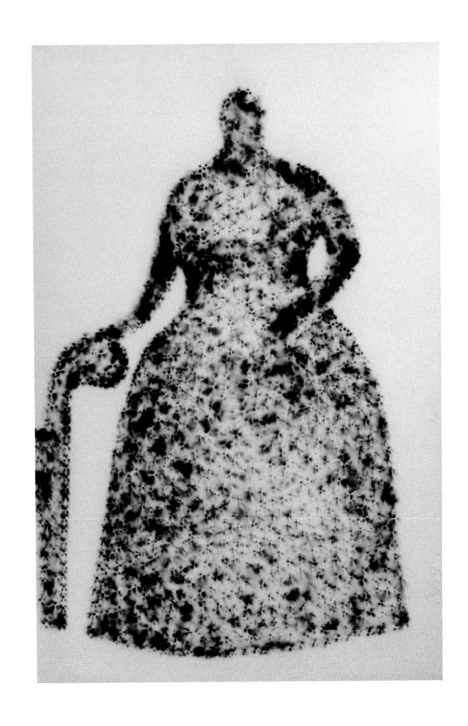

Lady in the Cook Photo 1971
Propane torch on crescent board

Lady in the Cook Photo 1971
Conte on handmade paper

Lady in the Cook Photo 1971
Compressed charcoal and eraser on Ingres
Arches MBM paper

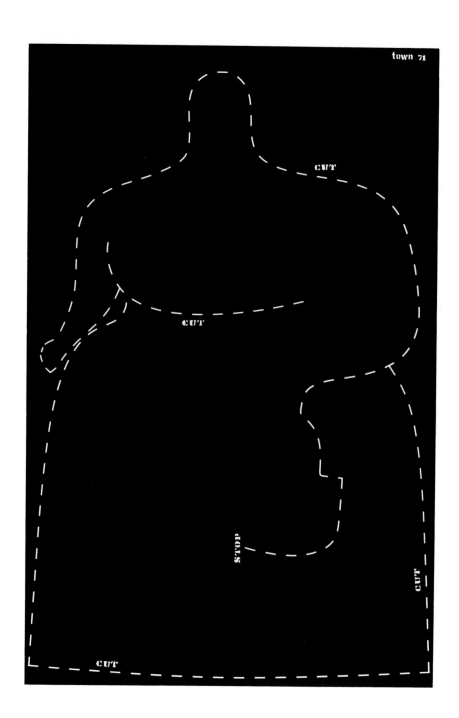

Lady in the Cook Photo 1971
Spray paint and tape, stencil and gouache on
crescent board

Lady in the Cook Photo 1971
Spray paint and tape on board

Lady in the Cook Photo 1971
Charcoal, pastel and white pencil crayon on
Ingres Arches paper

Park No. 1 1970
Oil and lucite on canvas

The Cook photograph – average, typical and yet, in its anonymity, lost – is open without violence to imaginative reformation. The photographs of the film stars are immediate and desired in a special way. "No matter," Town wrote in the introduction to his book *Silent Stars, Sound Stars, Film Stars,*

how oblique and tenuous the influence, film has been an integral part in the development of the lives of all of us in the western world.... As a child I had so much energy I crackled like a wire down in the street after a storm, yet the instant the curtain parted I was plugged in and my current flowed freely into another world.[6]

Although each drawing is individual in technique and graphic touch, their essential character lies in recalling both the image and the fantasy within the image. It is to capture a look, a glance, a movement – always fleeting, yet always fixed. Fidelity to the flashes of memory caught in the still photographs is vital, far more so than the seaming of the images into a film narrative.

That is particularly telling of Town's relationship to the art of his times. His very ability as a draughtsman and his love for drawing ("If I could do only one thing for the rest of my life, I'd draw.")[7] make him appear out of phase. For an artist working now, it is by drawing that he or she can most firmly manifest the continuity of history. Drawing, the essential reduction, loops through past and present; drawing denies novelty. The irony in Town's unchallenged ability to draw is that his drawings' roots in history keep them, as drawings, from being contentious.

Yet the continued appreciation of his ability to draw has been used as a screen to avoid the paintings. Eccentricity in drawing is not only acceptable but, in a sense, assumed. Eccentricity in painting, means standing against the mainstream, outside the normal bounds of seriousness. And once that determination is made, as in the minds of many it was for Town's paintings after 1965, the continuation of the mainstream makes it all but impossible to change its judgement. While I believe that the late 1960s was the least vital period for Town's *paintings*, the early 1970s saw the emergence of two major series of works – *Parks* and *Snaps* – that have not received proper critical consideration.

The *Parks* are some of the most evocative of Town's paintings, visual metaphors deeply embedded, both in concept and in pictorial structure, in the whole course of Town's work. They are, in their references and in their painterly expression, based on the conflict Town had so often expressed between the city and the landscape. When he exhibited the first three *Parks* in 1970, he spoke about how "any park is a miracle in this automated society."[8] The paintings show the gritty survival of a natural environment in surroundings that threaten to strangle it by defining small areas of richly impastoed colour and confining areas of flatly painted geometrically described shapes.

Park No. 5 1971
Oil and lucite on canvas

Untitled 1959-60
Oil and lucite on canvas

Park No. 9 1972
Oil and lucite on canvas

Park No. 6 1972
Oil and lucite on canvas

The series, of course, developed a variety of formal patterns, of size and format and of balance; but its essence was laid out in the first of the series, *Park No. 1* of 1970 (Ill. p. 161). The dark shape, formed by letters projected in perspective, oscillates in a positive-negative relationship with the surrounding area. The eccentricity of the shape and its sharply defined edges keep it in optical motion, as if its forceful imposition into the space depends on the ambiguity. The little area of bright, thick colour appears to be particularly stable, maintained by its strictly rectangular form within the curves and diagonals.

David Silcox has described the paintings as "parks in the midst of a man-made, over-ordered urban environment"[9] and links them to the work of the 1950s, particularly, the St. Lawrence Seaway mural of 1958, "where the whole work is a metaphor of the dam and its effect on the landscape." Reference can also be made to pictures such as *Harvest*[10] (Ill. p. 169) and, even more, to a painting such as *Interior Pitch Out* (Ill. p. 104) with its combination of even, open planes of colour and areas of bright, lively impasto. (This structure of combination is also found in many of the single autographic prints such as *The Dissident*.)

Two hundred years ago, William Pitt the Elder described the parks of London as the lungs of the city. The urban park is, however, an interesting reversal of the original idea of the park. The recreational park was initially a special area of land surrounding a major house or palace; this area, depending on national tradition, either extended order and rationality into nature, or established a contrast between architectural and natural order. One looked out at nature from the constructed centre of civilized order, from the finite to the infinite. The urban park reverses these roles; we look from nature to the encroachment of urban development, we look into the park to distance that encroachment. At another level of metaphor, it is the contrast between the naturalness of life, and how we construct around that naturalness. We "build" careers, we "form" opinions and relationships.

The very character of the *Park* paintings was set against the expectations of painting of the time. Areas of "expressionistic" painting are imposed on "cool" flat planes; geometric forms do not work as self-referential responses to the shape and form of the picture, but act idiosyncratically. The issue they raise as paintings, however, is not simply an opposition to work around him. Their origin lies in earlier paintings and in subject matter that had long concerned him. The constant testing of opposites in the *Parks* series is the same testing that lies at the base of his work in drawing, a reductive, abstract process, and in collage, an accumulative process.

In their strength of colour and shape and in their combinations of formal techniques, the *Snaps* are closely allied to the *Parks*. In some cases, such as *Snap 1975* (Ill. p. 173), there seems to be an inversion of the *Parks*, painted strong colours are set into the centre of the complex, textured "snapped" field.

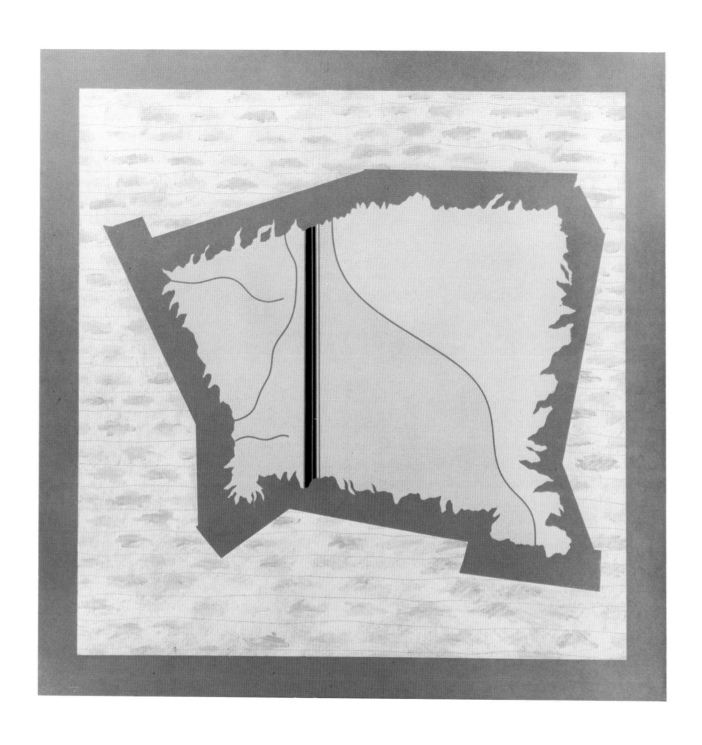

Park No. 17 1971-72
Oil and lucite on canvas

168

Harvest 1960
Oil and lucite on masonite

The name for the series came from the technique by which they were made. Town would load a length of string with thick paint, either by brushing it on, or squeezing it directly from the tube. Then, securing it taut across the canvas he would snap it against the canvas to transfer the paint. He had used the idea before, for instance, in the 1960 collage, *Ironic Keepsake* ; but he first used it as a device for organizing the composition of the St. Lawrence Seaway mural. As a technique for compositional organization, the 'Snap' has a very ancient pedigree. When straight lines were needed for borders and architecture in fresco paintings, a taut string was snapped against the damp plaster, leaving an indentation in it.[11]

The first of the *Snap* series comprised a small group of paintings in which narrow bands of snapped colours in two directions were set over a dark ground. Their effect, as in works such as *Snap No. 2* (Ill. p. 178), is like a prismatic breakdown of light emanating from the deep ground. The effect, with a dynamic impression of coloured light, is related to the *Silent Light* paintings that immediately preceded them. Town's control of the technique and his recognition of its potential led him rapidly to broaden the range of the paintings. During a period of three years or so he produced scores of paintings in the series. They range in size from a foot or eighteen inches square to *Snap*, 1975-76, which is five feet high and ten feet wide. As his technique developed, the surfaces became more complex in their colour mixtures, and denser in impasto as he built up layer on layer of paint. And with this density came ever greater possibilities of colour, not only by juxtaposition but also by the optical mixing of the tiny flecks of paint in multiple layers scattered from the impact of the loaded string on the surface. He would vary the proportions of the colours in certain sections so that, for instance, in one part he might use two "snaps" of a colour in a one-inch area; in another he might use four or six "snaps" of a single colour over the same distance. By these changes in proportion he could expand the effects of colour mixing in the eye. It was like inventing anew the massing of colours in the 1960 "fat" paintings.

I have mentioned the connection between the emergence of the *Snaps* and the *Silent Lights*. In another way they also develop aspects of the *Stretches*. The technique itself asserts the flatness *and* the materiality of the picture surfaces. The long, tense lines of the *Stretches*, defining the plane and direction of the surface, are like the strings. But in the *Snaps*, rather than contrasting a linearity against a uniform coloured ground, the lines themselves expand into both drawing and ground. What was implicit in the *Silent Lights* and *Stretches*, and earlier in paintings like *Fate Curtain* (Ill. p. 133), was brilliantly realized in the *Snaps*. The series was a direct challenge to all the talk generated by Greenberg about flatness and illusion. The core of the issue in the *Snaps* is that the paintings are totally flat and yet by the extension of colour by contrast and optical mixture the intimated pictorial space is vast and complex. Rather than progressively narrowing the possibilities of painting, or declining into "decoration pure and simple" (as Greenberg had earlier accused makers of collage), the *Snaps* were a means by which the essential character of painting was maintained but the possibilities of investigation became limitless.

Characteristically, however, a development or resolution of a proposal made in earlier works could not simply be left as a synthesis. The synthesis itself had to be overcome to assert a new and independent set of pictorial contrasts.

The very character of the technique demanded tightly ordered surfaces; the "snap" technique dictated an accumulation of straight lines. To work against this, in a sense to overcome his own development, he built the pictures in ways that would raise questions and inversions to the basic snapped structure. He would mask off areas and run the snap in contrasting directions; he would make circular forms as in *Snap No. 80* (Ill. p. 172), or irregular curved forms that counter the rigidity of the snap as in *Snap No. 86* (Ill. p. 174). Another direction was taken in the paintings he called "envelopes" or "double-envelopes", such as *Snap No. 79* (Ill. p. 177). By progressively masking out areas with oil resistant paper, he could form planes that apparently overlap.

As was earlier mentioned in the case of *Snap 36* the central area is painted with a flat surface. A contrast of techniques and textures is widely used. Sometimes the flatly painted surface is a major feature; in other cases, the emphasis on those areas is confined to the edges. A sort of *trompe l'oeil* effect is found in *Snap No. 66* and *Snap No. 80*. What seems to be photographers' colour and tone bars are imposed into the picture, in a witty comment on the colour structure of the paintings. Others, such as the massive *Snap 1975-6* and *In Memory of Emelio del Junco* (Ill. p. 176), have little or no modification of the snap surface, but exist by the attack of the colour alone, every colour being keyed up by the complexity of the paint structure.

In many respects the *Snaps* reclaim the range of painterly potential that Town had developed in the "expressionist" paintings of 1958 to 1960 and in the *Tyranny of the Corner* pictures of 1962-63 (Ill. p. 19 and pp. 106-107). With them he had developed a structure capable of bearing an infinite range of variation. They contained a discipline that both demanded conformity and yet remained inventively open. In this they differ sharply from the *Stretches* and *Silent Lights* and even from the *Parks* for those series are directed, and in a way restricted, by a particular range of pictorial and metaphorical possibilities. Essentially, the *Snaps* have an unlimited potential. They can be aggressive, as *In Memory of Emelio del Junco*; they can be elegant, such as *Snap 1975* (Ill. p. 173); they can work against what seems to be "right" for the technique, as in the curious but beautifully controlled red form in the centre of *Snap No. 66*. They can, as it were, turn the technique back on itself, as in the funny and crazy *Snap*

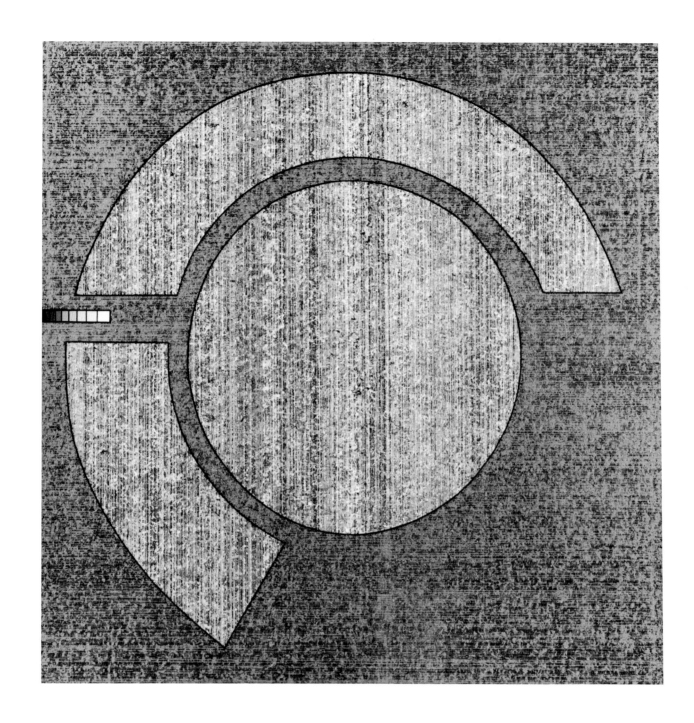

Snap No. 80 1974
Oil and lucite on canvas

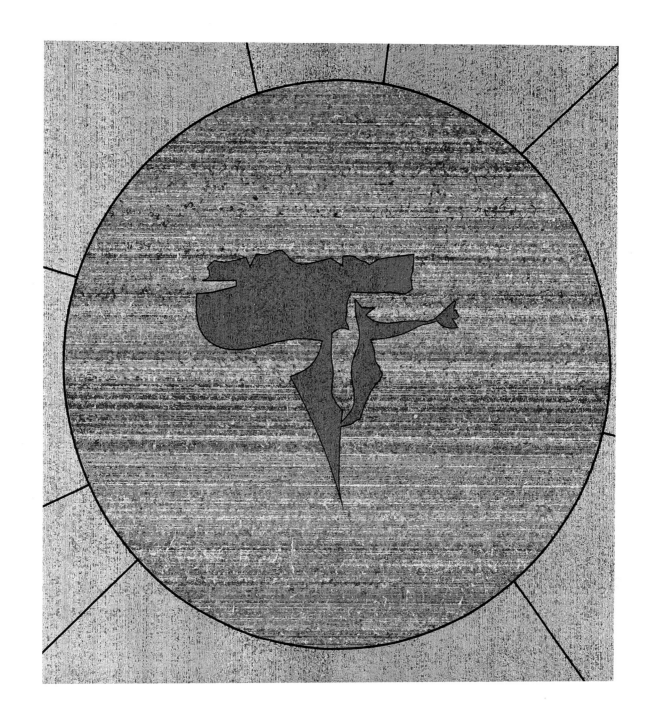

Snap 1975
Oil and lucite on canvas

Snap No. 86 1975
Oil and lucite on canvas

No. 86 (Ill. p. 174), in which the multi-coloured figure seems to be balanced on the tightrope of the red and blue lines as if they were paint-laden strings, anchored to the edge of the picture, waiting to be snapped.

The *Snaps* reasserted Town as a painter. But they were met, when shown in the 1970s, with general rejection or indifference. It is a situation due for revision; as Gary Michael Dault has recently said, "I now think they're among the most original, non-representative paintings ever made."[12] But in the mid-1970s the books, as it were, had been closed on Town.

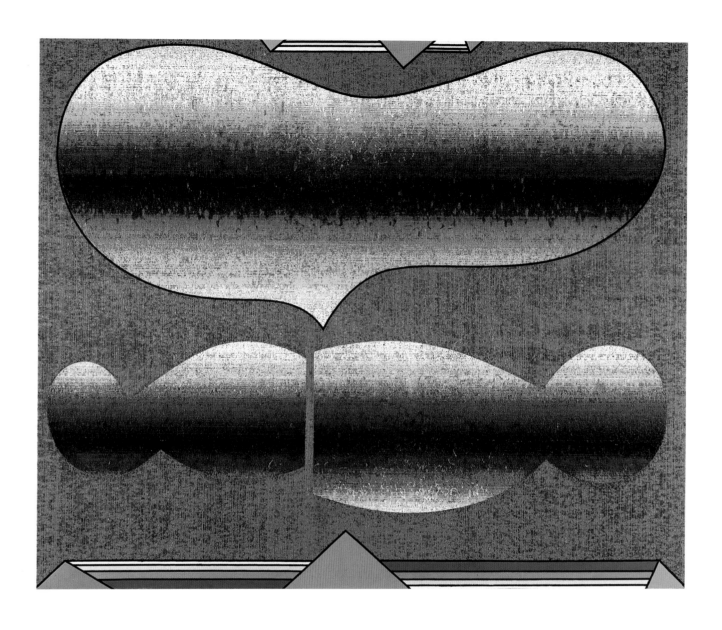

In Memory of Emelio del Junco 1974-75
Oil and lucite on canvas

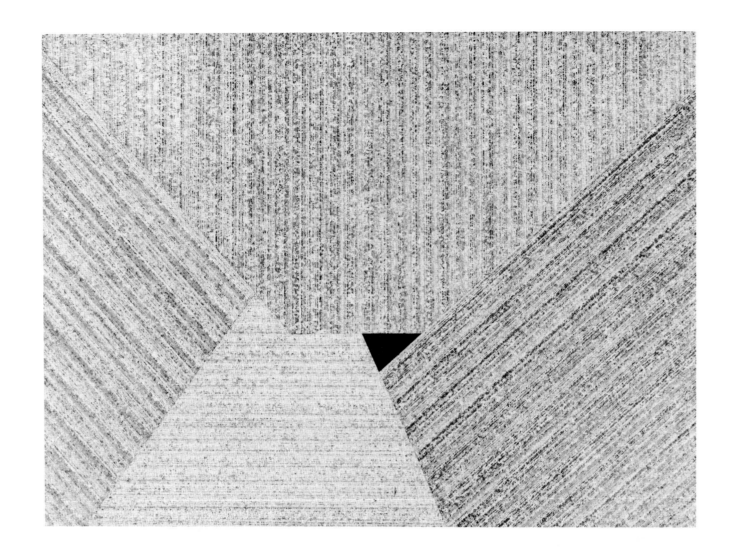

Snap No. 79 1975
Oil and lucite on canvas

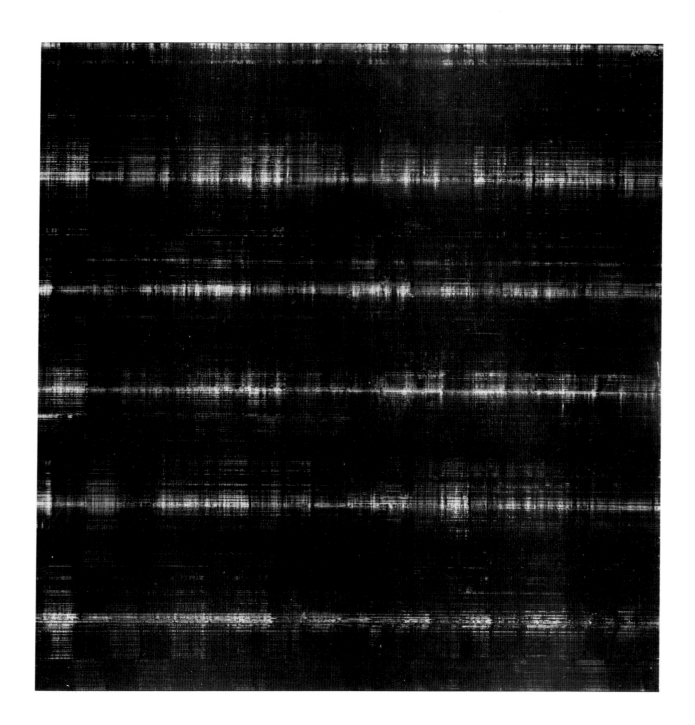

Snap No. 2 1972
Oil and lucite on canvas

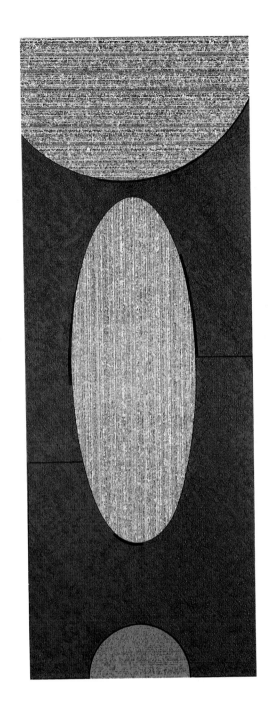

Snap 1975
Oil and lucite on canvas

SEVEN

It is now ten years since the Art Gallery of Windsor organized the exhibition *Indications: Harold Town 1944-1975*. It was the first major survey exhibition of Town's work to be mounted. One hundred and thirty paintings, collages, prints, sculptures and drawings were assembled, beginning with student work from the Ontario College of Art and concluding with paintings and drawings completed just months prior to the opening of the exhibition.[1] After its showing in Windsor, the exhibition went to the Sarnia Public Library and Art Gallery, slightly smaller due to space restrictions. It would have finished its course there had it not been for the efforts of a number of people, in particular Margaret Scrivener, then Minister of Government Services, to bring the exhibition to Toronto. It was shown at Macdonald Block, Queen's Park.[2]

Yet this exhibition, which should have been the opportunity for a major assessment of thirty years of Town's work, slipped quietly past. The point was not a matter of giving a senior artist "his due," but the fact of critical, that is measured response to the perspectives opened by an individual career of accomplishment within the context of recent Canadian art history. The perspective that the exhibition did garner was well expressed by Kay Kritzwiser. In reviewing the show for *The Globe and Mail* Kritzwiser asked:

Why should Town have to wait for Windsor to give him what amounts to a major retrospective? Why hasn't the National Gallery of Canada done it? (Is this a national scandal?) Why hasn't the Art Gallery of Ontario given the Toronto painter this distinction?[3]

She then sets out to answer her rhetorical question, and it goes to the core of the issue that the question had to be rhetorical:

'But he hasn't done anything important since the sixties.' That's a harsh answer but one camp believes it.... It betokens a frame of mind about Town which exists in some quarters official and private. I think it is unfortunate. I think part of it is Town's fault. Like so many thin-skinned people he has no concern for the thin skin of others. Unwittingly or not, he has built up a public image of Town the Flailer, hides flying as he flails. Perhaps he now runs into public resistance to Town's public image.

The opposition did not come from *public* resistance, but rather from resistance within the visual arts community, in which the "flail" had been most often exercised. Rather than face the work, it could be most effectively diminished by ignoring it or damning it with the faint praise that a decade or more earlier the artist had shown the promise of greatness. The whole issue was clearly summed up by Robert Fulford writing in 1980:

[Town] has insisted - rightly, in my view - on displaying not just one narrow strip of his sensibility but the entire range. Critics and curators, confronted with this plentitude, have sometimes turned away in nervous bewilderment. Somehow they know that an artist who does so many things

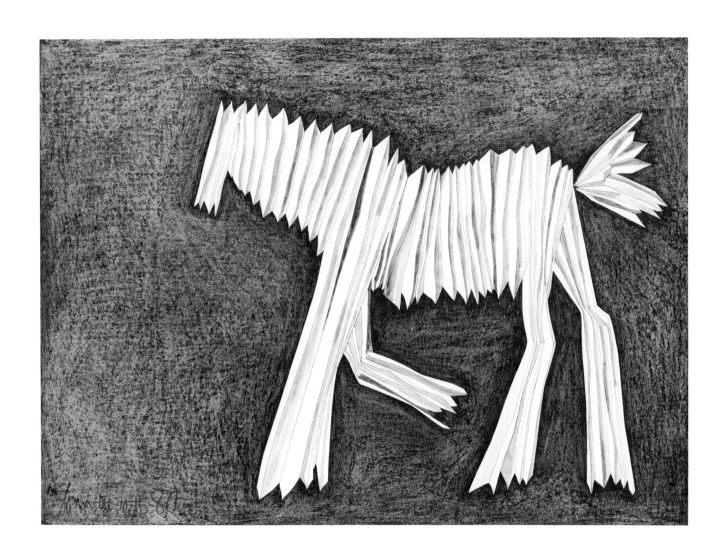

Toy Horse No. 141 1980
Ink, coloured pencil, pen and wash on paper

Toy Horse No. 192 1981
Collage, pen and ink, brush and ink, gouache,
wax resist and watercolour on camber sand
handmade paper

Toy Horse 1976
Pencil, oil pastel, lead pencil, pastel pencil on
coloured paper

can't be significantly good at any one of them. This conclusion requires that the critic or curator ignore the quality and authority of the work on the gallery walls; but that is seldom difficult, given practice.[4]

Ten years after the Windsor exhibition two things are clear. First, prevailing critical opinion has, with a few exceptions, remained unchanged. Second, Town has continued to work as vigorously as ever in painting, drawing, and collage.

But there are two constants, ultimately inseparable, in all the work he has done and continues to do. The structure of all that he has produced depends on the imposition of conflict and tension. Rather than defining a resolution, he takes the risk of irresolution that presses him to continue. These risks can take the form of throwing blocks in the way of the picture-making process; it may come as a reaction to work being made around him; it may come through his pursuit of a particular subject and its pictorial transformation. I have described this risk-taking in terms of contrasting drawing and collage – not simply as techniques but as opposing processes. Yet this contrast is not limited to the tensions within a particular work, for different aspects of those tensions occur in separate series of work being produced at the same time.

The second point also relates to dealing with conflict. On the one hand is Town's extroversion: opinionated, angry and sharp-witted, intolerant, and sometimes intemperate in his responses to what irritates him or who crosses him. On the other, is the obsessive introversion of his work; painting in the afternoon in the Studio Building, drawing at home into the early hours of the morning, working two or three days a week on collages. The tension arises out of conviction in his work and sensitivity to the responses it draws.

During the past ten years he has worked on a number of major series. There have been several series of drawings: the *God Drawings*, the *New Dining Room* drawings, the *Toy Horses*, begun in 1976 and comprising more than seven hundred individual works; the more recent *Bug Drawings*, and a series of pencil drawings still in progress called *The Famous*. There is one group of large-scale paintings on *Eccentrics* and a second series in progress called *Musclemen*. He is also working on a series of large three-dimensional assemblages.[5] His pace of exhibiting, while not as fervid as it was in the 1960s and early 1970s, continues strongly, as does the collection of his work. The response to the *Toy Horses* has been considerable.

Response to the new work by reviewers has been, in general, negative. Of the *Eccentric* paintings shown in 1981, one critic, while finding them very funny, wrote: "Harold Town has pulled off an amazing feat...[a] very large show of very bright, extremely clever paintings which are totally and uniformly mindless."[6]

Toy Horse No. 144 1980
Black ink and calligraphic pen on paper

Painting for Beatrice White — Winner of the
1912 Toronto Fly Killing Contest with a Score
of 543,360 dead insects 1980
Oil and lucite on canvas

Snowy Farr, the Demon Sweep of
Cambridgeshire 1980-81
Oil and lucite on canvas

Here, as often throughout his career, the usual initial response of reviewers to a new series has been to see it independent from previous work thereby rejecting the past for the delights of new toys. But Town's approach, in essence, does not break from the past. He began work on the *Toy Horse* drawings in 1976, almost immediately after ending the *Vale Variations* and stopping work on the *Snap* paintings.[7] The *Vale Variations* were based on Florence Vale's drawing, *Pyramid of Roses*, 1965; the *Toy Horse* drawings were inspired by a toy horse acquired from an antique store. The *Snap* paintings had developed from that single technical idea that, critically directed against the character and procedures of post-painterly abstraction, quickly opened a new range of potential in abstract painting.

The paintings of the early 1980s have the playful inventiveness of the *Toy Horses* and the punchy colour (as if to say never leave a possibility languishing in the tube). The large-size paintings are on two subject themes: the *Musclemen*, which respond perhaps to the seriousness with which the muscles of new figurative painting are being flexed; and another series recounting the adventures of eccentrics. Even with their "impossible" subjects and long descriptive titles, they are not "mindless," but a way of bridging the gap between the conceptual seriousness of art (and the talk that goes with it) and the results represented in painting. The satire on art strikes at both the foolishness of fashion and the distinction between the consistent values of art and their etiolation. The explicit description in the titles – *The Art Establishment changes from Matisse to Picasso Time* (Ill. p. 190) and *The Shade of Albert Franck returns disguised as Rembrandt to fan the platitudes of Post-Painterly Abstraction drying on the Greenberg Line* (Ill. p. 189) – simply underlines the pretentious assumption of so much expected from so little. (The second title recalls a much earlier satire on the hook-line-and-sinker attitude followed by formalist criticism and art, the painting *Sculpture reaching for the High Painting Line* of 1960.)

As if to counter his contempt for the knee-jerk of "authorized" art, he paints in a similar style a group of pictures that, in an exaggerated way, assert an individuality so far outside conventional thought and behaviour that we must make a special category for it, that of the eccentric. Thus there is *The Reverend Evan Sedgemore blowing his bugle under water*, and the historian Oswald Spengler in *Spengler writing "The Decline of the West" at his desk on top of the kitchen table* (Ill. p. 192). His room is equipped with a black light bulb and red rays that contain an embryonic Nazi flag, referring to the Nazis' adoption of Spengler's historical speculations to their version of historical determinism. There is also the intrepid Charles Waterton, an early nineteenth-century taxidermist who thought he had found a way to utilize Niagara Falls, as a giant whirlpool for healing: *Charles Waterton (1782-1865) attempts to cure his sprained ankle in the "tremendous cascade" of Niagara Falls* (Ill. p. 191).

*The Shade of Albert Franck returns disguised
as Rembrandt to fan the Platitudes of
Post-Painterly Abstraction drying on the
Greenberg line* 1979-80
Oil on Belgian linen

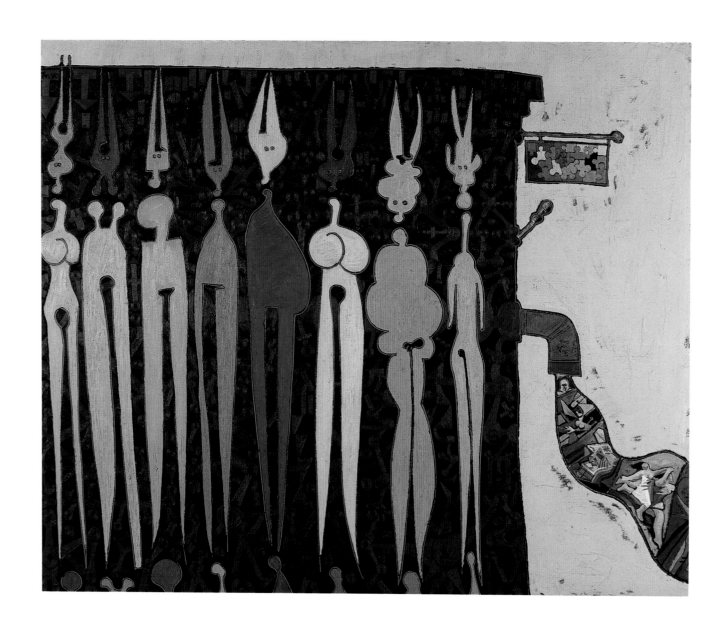

Art Establishment changes from Matisse to
Picasso Time 1980
Oil and lucite on canvas

Charles Waterton (1782-1865) attempts to
cure his sprained ankle in the "tremendous
cascade" of Niagara Falls 1980
Oil and lucite on canvas

Spengler writing The Decline of the West *at his desk on top of the kitchen table* 1980
Oil and lucite on canvas

In his current work, as throughout his career, he pursues the different demands and capacities of painting and drawing and collage/assemblage, and any proper assessment of his work must account for the relations between the various fronts on which he works simultaneously. To isolate one element while ignoring the others is, at best, poor criticism and, at worst, forcing an artist into one's image of an artist. Currently he is working on the paintings of the *Musclemen* (Ill. pp. 6-7 and p. 201), the drawings of *The Famous* (Ill. p. 9 and pp. 204-211), and the large-scale assemblages. They are critical, nostalgic and satirical; they are also deeply integrated with his previous work.

The *Musclemen* are, in a way, curious icons of our time, richly painted displays of display calling upon the traditions of figure painting and of ideal beauty, but splitting physical and intellectual perfection apart and, having to accept that one cannot put muscles on head, hands and feet, using the rest of their bodies for competitive entertainment – the individual as a commodity. The drawings of *The Famous*, by contrast, are reinvestments in the past. Made with an F pencil on white acid-free board from photographs of writers, musicians, film stars, a Queen – Victoria (Ill. p. 210) – and a politician – Lincoln (Ill. p. 207) – they reclaim abstraction with the touch of a pencil line. They are related particularly in their subjects to the *Silent Stars, Sound Stars, Film Stars* series, but whereas those drawings often had the loose flickering quality of the movie screen, *The Famous* have a still, almost lost character, fixed by the clarity of a profile or a detail of drapery. The assemblages are funny, busy satires on our dependence on and deference to specialization in *The Weather Report (A Paean to Inaccuracy)* (Ill. p. 195); the relationship between "success" and its purpose in *Canadian Retirement Dream* (Ill. p. 203); the values of the discussion of art in *Mondrian and Pollock Memorial No. 3* (Ill. p. 194); or the confusion of meaning in *All Symbols are Signs All Signs are Symbols* (Ill. p. 197), which combines a brass rubbing with rubber automobile splash guards.

The variety in Town's work and the simultaneous work on forms and directions that appear unrelated often have been dismissed glibly as Town's inability to settle on one thing. However, consistency does not lie in piping the same tune the same way, but in responding to the contrasts and conflicts of circumstances. His criticism and satire not only challenge thin and pretentious attitudes, but sets against it his work, the results of his constant challenge to himself. There is stubbornness and obsessiveness, but it is without duplicity; he does not conceal what he does any more than he can suppress his challenge to witlessness, to his contempt for so much talk about so little art presented in the hope that inscrutability will be mistaken for profundity.

The critical sniping at Town is easy – he presents a large target. But it is also, finally, insignificant, for the work exists. A different sort of critical

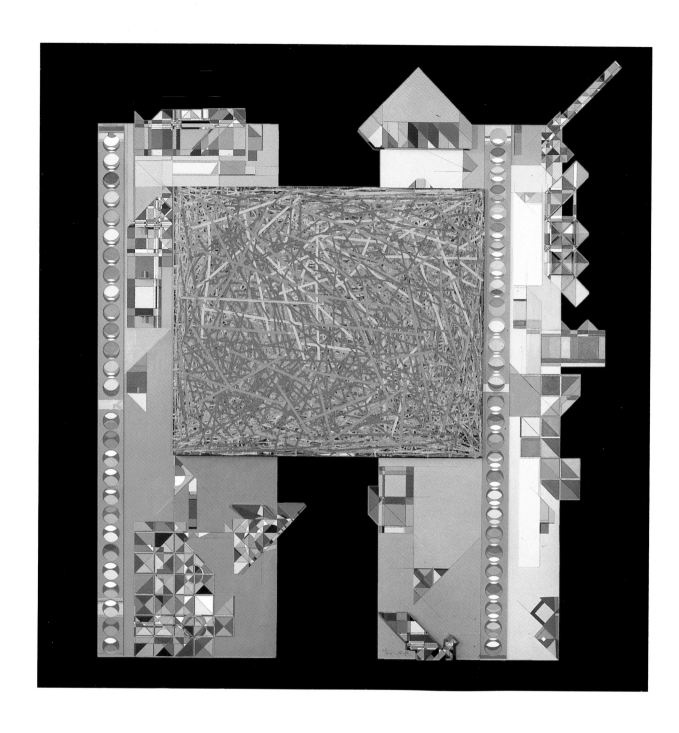

Mondrian and Pollock Memorial No. 3
1975-85
Collage

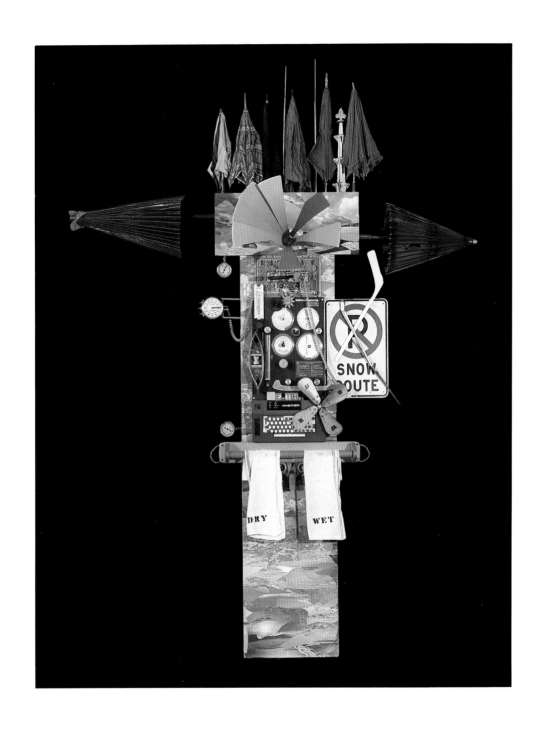

The Weather Report (A Paean to Inaccuracy)
1984-85
Collage

Tomorrow Doorway 1985
Collage

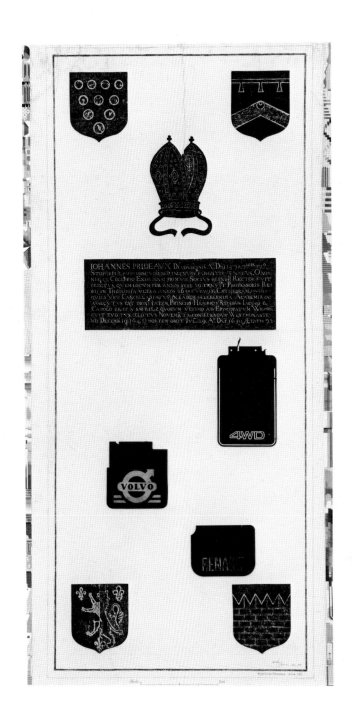

All Symbols are Signs, All Signs are Symbols
1967-85
Collage

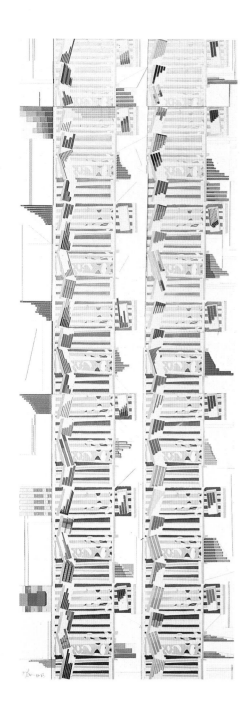

Modern Times Print Out 1981-85
Collage

Time Centre 1984-85
Collage

assessment was that recalled by Joan Murray when, in regard to the *Eccentric* paintings of 1981, she looked back on the historical reasons for Town's recent reputation:

Instead of being 'the touchstone for the development of art in the country as a whole,' as critics used to call him, he became an outsider, as beyond the pale as any of the eccentrics who are the subject of his work today.[8]

This raises two issues. First, Town has *always* been an outsider. Self-described as such in the early 1950s, it was expressed in the very direction he took and expressed pictorially during the Painters Eleven years. If he was lionized in the early 1960s, and responded to it, nothing he has done, said, or written runs counter to the position he formed as a very young artist.

Second, the notion that he or any other individual could be "the touchstone for the development of art in the country as a whole" is simply evidence – and pathos-ridden evidence at that – of the cultural poverty of "the country as a whole." It reveals a desire less for achievement than for the complacent security of institutions, raising them so to abuse them, while expecting their support as a right.

If Town is to be thought of as a touchstone of anything it is by his very refusal to represent himself as an abstract notion of a cultural property. Where his example lies is in his absolute commitment to his work, his criticism – pictorial, verbal, written – and his independence. And in this lies the impossibility of a school of influence trailing behind him, a fact that arises, at least in part, from the situation of art within the Toronto in which he grew up.

The radical position of the Group of Seven lay precisely in their belief in founding a "touchstone for the development of art in the country as a whole," a belief that they collectively, and by their influence, pursued with exemplary success. The malaise in Toronto art in the early 1950s was not due to a lack of direction but because the direction that did exist had gained the status of an institution. Town's contribution then and later is that he has refused the status of an institution. And if he must bear others' disappointment and criticism of that refusal, it is finally a mark of his importance. He is a great Canadian artist because he would never accept to be *the* great Canadian artist.

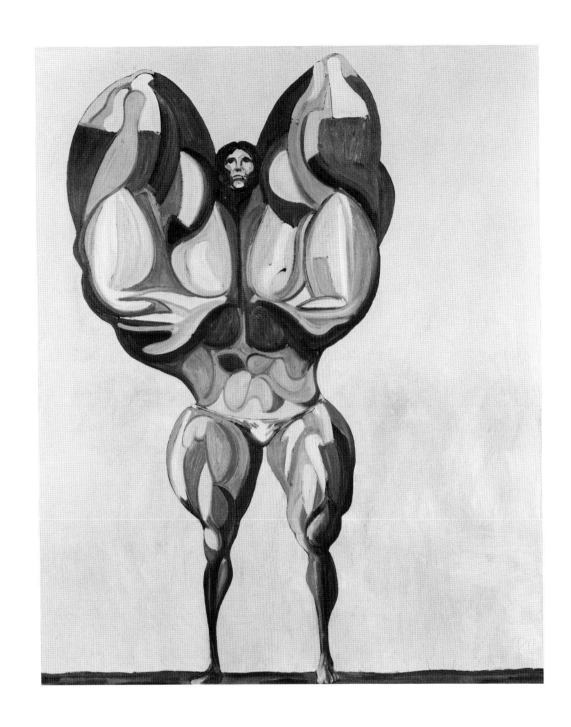

Muscleman 1984
Oil and lucite on canvas

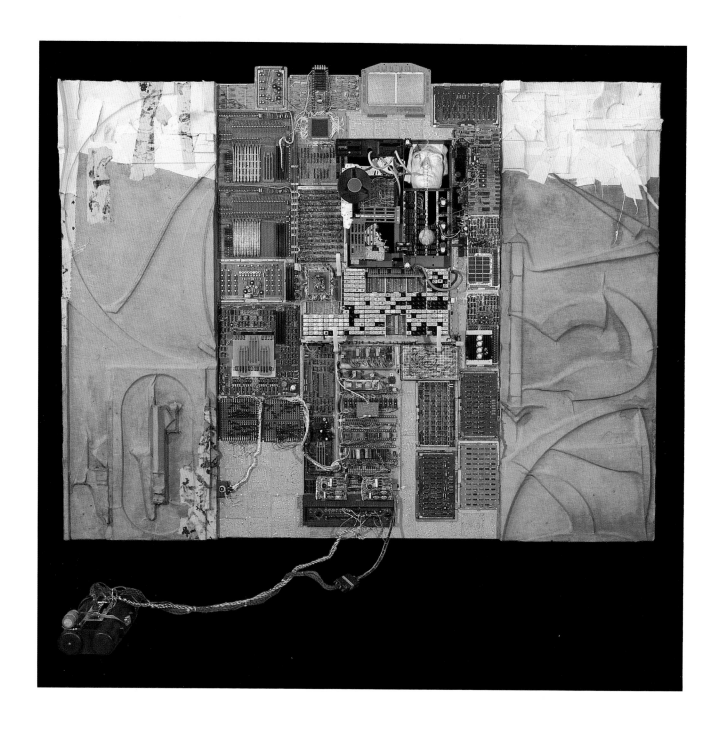

Yesterday, Today and Tomorrow 1940-85
Collage

Canadian Retirement Dream 1982-85
Collage

Piet Mondrian 1942 1985
Pencil on acid-free matt board

Lon Chaney, The Phantom of the Opera,
Universal 1925 1984
Pencil on acid free matt board

Your Tooth in my neck — released as "The
Fearless Vampire Killers" "Dance of the
Vampires" Roman Polanski 1967 1985
Pencil on acid-free matt board

Abraham Lincoln, Nov. 8, 1863, Washington,
D.C. 1985
Pencil on acid-free matt board

Oskar Kokoshka draws Ezra Pound 1985
Pencil on acid-free matt board

Stephane Mallarme 1842-98 1985
Pencil on acid-free matt board

Queen Victoria 1897 1985
Pencil on acid-free matt board

Rasputin with Upper Class Ladies 1916 1985
Pencil on acid-free matt board

NOTES

INTRODUCTION

1. Robert Fulford, "Introduction," *Poets and Other People. Drawings by Harold Town* (Windsor, Art Gallery of Windsor, 1980), p. 6.

2. "Harold Town" *Canadian Art* (Spring 1986) p. 45.

ONE

1. Renato Pogglioli, *The Theory of the Avant-Garde* (New York: Harper & Row, 1971), p.9. Gabriel-Désiré Laverdant, a follower of the utopian socialist Charles Fourier, wrote *De la mission de l'art et du rôle des artistes*.

2. The situation was, of course, a complex one, as the debate within the Automatiste movement showed. See in particular François-Marc Gagnon, *Paul-Émile Borduas (1905-1960) Biographie critique et analyse de l'oeuvre* (Montréal: Fides, 1978).

3. The expansion in population refers to the Metropolitan area. The City proper lost population between 1951 and 1956 and after 1961, while the suburban areas grew rapidly. See Anthony H. Richmond, *Immigrants and Ethnic Groups in Metropolitan Toronto* (Toronto: Institute for Behavioural Research, York University, 1967), p. 1.

4. On the history of New York's cultural hegemony, see the excellent study by Serge Guilbault, *How New York Stole the Idea of Modern Art* (Chicago and London: The University of Chicago Press, 1983).

5. Rodolphe de Repentigny, "Le Groupe des Onze," *Vie des Arts* Numéro 12 (automne 1958), pp. 27-33. Repentigny (1926-1959), who painted under the pseudonym Jauran and formed *Les Plasticiens* in 1954, wrote for the magazine *L'Autorité* (under the name of François Bourgogne) and was art writer for *La Presse* (Montreal) from 1952 to 1959.

6. See Donald Goudy, "One-Man War against Modern Art" *The Star Weekly*, August 20, 1955.

7. At a meeting on May 9, 1957 the group agreed not to participate in "a larger society show." Town, Bush, Hodgson, Nakamura, and Yarwood boycotted the 1958 OSA Exhibition, but individual participation in society shows did continue.

8. Archibald Barnes quoted in Rose Macdonald, "Is Art Revolution Here or Is It a Doodling Phase," *The Toronto Telegram*, 9 March 1951, p. 3.

9. *Ibid.*

10. *Ibid.*

11. As recorded in the files of The Robert McLaughlin Gallery; see Joan Murray, *Painters Eleven in Retrospect* (Oshawa: The Robert McLaughlin Gallery, 1979), p. 69.

12. Mead continued to exhibit with the group and was active in bringing together Montreal and Toronto artists.

13. Murray, *op. cit.*, p. 10.

14. The two exhibitions were at The Stable Gallery, The Montreal Museum of Fine Arts, 8-30 April 1960 and Kitchener-Waterloo Art Gallery, 2 December 1960 – 15 January 1961.

15. Murray *op. cit.*, pp. 73-77.

16. See, for instance, Elizabeth Kilbourn, "The Greenberg Gospel," *Toronto Star*, February 22, 1964 and Barry Lord, *The History of Painting in Canada: Towards a People's Art*, (Toronto, NC Press, 1974), p. 208.

17. Lord, *op. cit.*

18. Vincent Tovell, "Eleven Painters Start a War," *Canadian Commentator* (November 1957), p. 10.

19. Rodolphe de Repentigny, "Deux excellents peintres canadiens," *La Presse* (Montreal), March 1957.

TWO

1. Pearl McCarthy, "Art and Artists," *The Globe and Mail* (Toronto), February 1954.

2. Notably the *Canadian Abstract Exhibition*, which was organized by Alexandra Luke in 1952, and opened at the YWCA (Adelaide House), Oshawa and was circulated during the next year to Windsor, London, Toronto (Hart House), Peterborough, Hamilton, Montreal, and Sackville, NB. Also the *Unaffiliated Artists Exhibitions*, organized by Albert Franck and R.F. Valkenberg, at The Fine Art Galleries, Eaton's College Street in the early 1950s.

3. Reprinted in Kay Woods, *A History of Painters Eleven*, (Oshawa: The Robert McLaughlin Gallery, 1970), n.p.

4. Murray, *op. cit.*, p. 10.

5. See, for instance, Diana Nemiroff, "*Les Plasticiens* and the Painters Eleven: Roots of Canadian Modernism," *Vanguard*, vol. 10, no. 7 (September 1981), p. 23.

6. See *Indications. Harold Town 1944-1975*, (Windsor: Art Gallery of Windsor, 1975). no. 10.

7. William Heine, "Points of View Make a Lively Show," *Weekend Magazine*, vol. 8, no. 45 (1958), pp. 6, 17.

8. For Cahén's life and work see David Burnett, *Oscar Cahén* (Toronto: Art Gallery of Ontario, 1983).

9. See, for instance, Paul Duval, *Four Decades: The Canadian Group of Painters and their Contemporaries 1930-1970* (Toronto: Clarke, Irwin, 1972), p. 135.

10. Cahén first exhibited a painting at the 75th Annual Exhibition of the Ontario Society of Artists in 1947.

11. The Town work is dated 1953 and was shown in February 1954; *Vivid Structure* was first shown in May 1954.

12. Robert Fulford, "The Multiplicity of Harold Town," *artscanada*, vol. 28, no. 2 (April-May 1971), pp. 49-56.

13. Barrie Hale, "Out of the Park: Modernist Painting in Toronto, 1950-1980," *Provincial Essays*, vol. 2 (Toronto : Phacops Publishing Society, 1985), p. 39.

14. *Ibid.*

15. He showed at the Laing Galleries in 1960.

16. Mead was forced to stop painting for medical reasons; in the intervening years he concentrated on drawing and photography.

THREE

1. No count or full catalogue of the prints has ever been made. The inscriptions on the prints do not always refer to the date of

their making. Quite often he would sign and date prints only when they went out on exhibition.

2. John Elderfield, *Kurt Schwitters* (New York and London: Thames and Hudson, 1985), p. 90.

3. Meyer Schapiro, "The Apples of Cézanne: An Essay on the Meaning of Still Life," (1968) in *Modern Art, 19th and 20th Centuries: Selected Papers* (New York: ?, 1978), p. 19. (Quoting from George H. Mead, *The Philosophy of the Act* (1938.)

4. Natalie Sarraulte, *Prière d'insérer*, in Ann Jefferson, *The nouveau roman and the poetics of fiction* (Cambridge: Cambridge University Press, 1980), p. 41.

5. Guiseppe Balsamo (1743-1795) of Palermo was one of the players in the Diamond Necklace Scandal of 1784-86, which implicated Queen Marie Antoinette and the Cardinal de Rohan.

6. The Haiku form, originally a comic poem, was given new dignity in the late seventeenth century by Matsuo Basho.

7. Harold Town and David Silcox, *Tom Thomson* (Toronto: McClelland and Stewart, 1977). Town rejects absolutely Barry Lord's statement "…his comparisons of his colour and texture to those of Tom Thomson"; see Barry Lord, *op. cit.* p. 206.

8. The first English exhibition of both artists was a two-person show at the Arthur Tooth Gallery in London in 1958.

9. Borduas was subsequently less than generous regarding the impact that Pellan's work had on him; Marian Scott spoke of the "explosive effect on Montreal" that Pellan's work had and the critic Paul Dumas referred to it as "a blood transfusion."

10. Clement Greenberg, "Collage," *Modern Art and Modernism: A Critical Anthology* (New York: Harper & Row, 1982), p. 107. First published as "The pasted-paper revolution," *Art News* (September 1958), pp. 46-49, 60.

11. Elderfield, *op. cit.*

12. Letter to Evan Turner, 26 April 1960. Files of the Montreal Museum of Fine Arts.

13. Robert Musil, *Young Törless*, trans. Eithne Wilkins and Ernst Kaiser (New York: Pantheon Books, 1955), p. 160.

14. "Toronto's Beauty Enthralls Painter," *The Toronto Telegram*, 16 November 1960.

15. *Robert Motherwell* (Buffalo: Albright-Knox Art Gallery and New York: Abbeville Press, 1983), p. 16.

16. "We Love Toronto Because," *Chatelaine*, vol. 51, no. 8 (August 1, 1978), p. 36.

FOUR

1. "Toronto School Kids Exposed to Filthy Painting," *Flash* (Toronto), 22 December 1951.

2. Robert Fulford, "What's New in the Arts," *Chatelaine*, August 1958.

3. Pearl McCarthy, "Town and his country: the realm of power and the river," *The Globe Magazine* 25 October 1958.

4. The Gallery closed in 1959 because the building it was in was to be demolished.

5. Barbara Moon, "The Overnight Bull Market in Modern Painting," *Maclean's*, vol. 74, no. 24, December 2, 1961, pp. 222-23.

6. Town and Elizabeth Mayhew represented Canada at the 1964 Venice Biennale.

7. Moon, *op. cit.*

8. Robert Fulford, "World of Art," *Toronto Star*, 26 February 1961.

9. Pearl McCarthy, *The Globe and Mail* (Toronto), 4 March 1961.

10. A group of artists who showed at the Greenwich Gallery and the Isaacs Gallery included Michael Snow, Joyce Wieland, Dennis Burton, Graham Coughtry, Richard Gorman, Gordon Rayner, John Meredith, and Robert Markle.

11. *The Toronto Telegram*, 24 October 1964.

12. *The Toronto Telegram*, 28 August 1965, p. 23.

13. Paul Duval, *The Toronto Telegram*, 21 March 1964.

14. Harry Malcolmson, *The Toronto Telegram*, 26 February 1966, p. 10.

15. Robert Fulford, "Books: Cancult," *Toronto Star*, 19 January 1961.

16. See Harold Town, *Enigmas* (Toronto: McClelland and Stewart, 1965). The *Maclean's* article appeared under the title "To Canada with Love and Hisses," January 23, 1965.

17. Barrie Hale, "Introduction," in *Toronto Painting: 1953-1965*, (Ottawa: National Gallery of Canada, 1972), p. 22.

18. Kildaire Dobbs, "Eros on Yonge Street," *Saturday Night*, February 1966, p. 19.

19. Hale, *op. cit.*

20. Duval, *op. cit.*

21. Dennis Reid, *A Concise History of Canadian Painting* (Toronto: Oxford University Press, 1973), p. 289.

22. Hale, *op. cit.*, pp. 69-70.

23. Barry Lord, *The History of Painting in Canada: Towards a People's Art* (Toronto, NC Press, 1974), p. 206.

24. "Perspective," *Toronto Star*, 9 February 1963.

25. "A Critical Tour of the Art Galleries," *New York Herald Tribune*, 17 October 1964; "Art: This Week's Shows Summarized," *New York Times*, 24 October 1964.

26. "Around the Galleries," *Time*, New York, 16 October 1964.

27. Paul Duval, "No Scratch and Dribble," *The Toronto Telegram*, 26 September 1959.

28. Algernon Charles Swinburne, *Laus Veneris*.

29. Gary Michael Dault, "Paint : From rapture to rancour, an anatomy of the medium," *Canadian Art*, Fall 1984, p. 46.

30. Trent Frayne, "John C. Parkin : Canada's bright architectural star," *Toronto Star*, 9 January 1965.

FIVE

1. *Imperial Oil Review*, October 1962.

2. See "Reminiscences by Jack Bush," interview with Jack Bush by Lesley Fry and John Newton in *Jack Bush: A Retrospective* (Toronto: Art Gallery of Ontario, 1976), n.p.

3. See Jacques Barzun, *Classic, Romantic and Modern* (Chicago and London: The University of Chicago Press, 1961), p. 23.

4. See, for instance, Barbara Haskell, *Blam ! The Explosion of Pop, Minimalism, and Performance 1958-1964* (New York: Whitney Museum of American Art, 1984).

5. Reprinted in *Meditations on a Hobby Horse* (London: Phaidon Press, 1971), pp. 151-161.

6. Elizabeth Kilbourn, *Toronto Star*, 14 April 1962.

7. The one exception to this was a small show at the Bendale Branch of the Scarborough Public Library in April and May 1865. He continued to show works on paper in Canada and was included in a substantial number of group exhibitions.

8. Pearl McCarthy, *The Globe and Mail* (Toronto), October 1948.

9. Harry Malcolmson, "Introduction," *Paintings 1964; Paintings 1965* (Toronto: Mazelow Gallery and Jerrold Morris International Gallery, 1966), n.p.

10. *Ibid.*

11. *Indications, op. cit.*, no. 56.

SIX

1. A group of the last series was published as *Silent Stars, Sound Stars, Film Stars*, with an introduction by the artist (Toronto: McClelland and Stewart, 1971).

2. *Indications, op. cit.*, no. 83.

3. "The Angriest Canadian," *Chicago Tribune Sunday Magazine*, 5 February 1967, p. 34.

4. The early drawings of the series were published in a limited edition as *Harold Town Enigmas* (Toronto: McClelland and Stewart, 1964).

5. Roland Barthes, *Camera Lucida*, trans. Richard Howard (New York: Hill and Wang, 1981), pp. 27, 43, 45.

6. *Silent Stars, Sound Stars, Film Stars, op. cit.*, p. 11.

7. "Paint with your feet, upside down, says Harold Town," *Kitchener-Waterloo Record*, February 1973.

8. Paul Russell, "Artist Harold Town through Three Styles," *Toronto Star*, 5 December 1970.

9. *Harold Town: First Exhibition of New Work, 1969-1973*, (Oshawa: The Robert McLaughlin Gallery, 1973) n.p.

10. See *Indications*, 1975, no. 57.

11. The technique of fresco painting, properly speaking, is painting on an area of plaster that is still damp. The paint is absorbed into the surface and, through the chemical changes in the drying process, form a permanent bond with the support.

12. "Harold Town and Gary Michael Dault: A Dialogue," 1985.

SEVEN

1. The exhibition was curated by Ted Fraser who also prepared the exhibition catalogue notes. The catalogue listed 131 items, two of which were not shown.

2. Six works from the Windsor listing were omitted but others from the artist's collection were added. A check list of the exhibition, reproducing the Windsor catalogue entries, was published by the Ministry of Government Services.

3. Kay Kritzwiser, "Town: from innovation to proficiency short on heart," *The Globe and Mail*, 11 October 1975, p. 31.

4. Robert Fulford, *Poets and Other People: Drawings By Harold Town* (Windsor: The Art Gallery of Windsor, 1980), p. 6.

5. This listing omits work continued on series like the *Vale Variations* and *French Postcards* begun before 1975, on a much wider range of figurative and abstract paintings and on small collages and assemblages.

6. John Bentley Mays, " 'Garage Sale' good for a laugh," *The Globe and Mail*, 16 May 1981, p. 13.

7. The *Snaps* were stopped for medical reasons; the continual action of drawing and snapping the strings injured Town's shoulder.

8. Joan Murray, "Galleries: Himself Surprised," *Toronto Calendar Magazine*, June 1981, p. 46.

WRITINGS BY THE ARTIST

Statement on invitation to *Painters Eleven*. Toronto: Roberts Gallery, 11-26 February 1955.

Statement written for *Painters Eleven, 1957*. Toronto: The Park Gallery, 31 October-16 November 1957.

Introduction to catalogue *Painters Eleven with Ten Distinguished Artists from Quebec, October 31st to November 15th, 1958*. Toronto: The Park Gallery.

"Introduction." *Oscar Cahén Memorial Exhibition* held concurrently with the *87th Annual Exhibition: The Ontario Society of Artists, March 21st to April 19th, 1959*. Art Gallery of Toronto.

"Toronto's Beauty Enthralls Painter." *The Toronto Telegram*, 16 November 1960.

In "18 Print-makers." Ed. Elizabeth Kilbourn. *Canadian Art*, March/April 1961, pp. 110-111.

Enigmas. Toronto: McClelland and Stewart, 1964.

"Thoughts for St. Valentine." *Saturday Night*, February 1967, pp. 30-34.

In "New Style in Town." *Time*, November 14, 1969.

"He's been Here All Along." Introductory essay to catalogue *The Vanishing City: An Exhibition of Paintings by Albert Jacques Franck*, York University, March 9 & 10, 1963. Reprinted by Gallery Moos in catalogue *Albert Jacques Franck*, 1970.

Silent Stars, Sound Stars, Film Stars. Toronto: McClelland and Stewart, 1971.

"Note to critics: light bulbs have no lesson for sun." *The Globe and Mail*, 25 November 1972.

"Letter to the Editor." *The Globe and Mail*, 1 December 1972.

"Foreword." *Josef Drenters Retrospective*. Oakville: Oakville Centennial Gallery, 1972.

"Sinews of an Ideal Critic." *The Globe and Mail*, 5 May 1973, p. 37.

"Drawing is One Way to give a Girl a Good Line." *Art Magazine*, Fall 1973, pp. 22-24.

Essay in *A Tribute to Albert Franck*. Art Gallery of Ontario, October 19-November 11, 1973.

"This leg has a hollow sound." *The Globe and Mail*, 17 November 1973.

Albert Franck: Keeper of the Lanes. Toronto: McClelland and Stewart, 1974.

"The prune and other artful remembrances." *Weekend Magazine*, 8 January 1977.

Tom Thomson: The Silence and the Storm. (with David P. Silcox). Toronto: McClelland and Stewart, 1977.

"A Child's Enchantment with the Tree." *The Citizen* (Ottawa), December 24, 1985, p. A8.

OTHER WRITERS

Allen, Helen. "Jack of All Trades: Hydro Mural Painter Proves It." *The Toronto Telegram*, 3 September 1958.

Art Gallery of Windsor. *Indications: Harold Town: 1944-75*. Windsor: Art Gallery of Windsor, 1975.

Barnes, Archibald and Macdonald, Manly. "Is Art Revolution Here or Is It a Doodling Phase." *The Toronto Telegram*, 9 March 1951, p. 3.

Burnett, David. "Harold Town delivers what the censors wouldn't." *The Citizen* (Ottawa), 7 December 1973.

_____. *Oscar Cahén*. Toronto: Art Gallery of Ontario, 1983.

_____ and Marilyn Schiff. *Contemporary Canadian Art*. Edmonton: Hurtig Publishers, 1983.

Chandler, John Noel. "Drawing Reconsidered." *artscanada*, October/November 1970.

Dault, Gary Michael. "Paint. From rapture to rancour, an anatomy of the medium." *Canadian Art*, Fall 1984, p. 46.

_____. "Harold Town." *Canadian Art*. Spring 1986, pp. 45-53.

Dexter, Gail. "They love Harold Town – in Chicago." *Toronto Star*, 19 April 1969.

Dobbs, Kildaire. "Eros on Yonge Street." *Saturday Night*, February 1966, p. 19.

Duval, Paul. *Four Decades. The Canadian Group of Painters and their Contemporaries 1930-1970*. Toronto: Clarke, Irwin, 1972.

_____. "Town Goes to Town." *The Toronto Telegram*, 21 March 1964.

_____. "No Scratch and Dribble." *The Toronto Telegram*, 26 September 1959.

Fulford, Robert. "What's New in the Arts." *Chatelaine*, August 1958.

_____. "Town Works Score 'Musical' Success." *Toronto Star*, 31 January 1959.

_____. "Art yahoos laugh in ignorance." *Toronto Star*, 14 February 1959.

_____. "Books. Cancult." *Toronto Star*, 19 January 1961.

_____. "Jungle for heroes." *Toronto Star*, 25 February 1961, p. 30.

_____. "The mysteries of Town." *Toronto Star*, 17 December 1964.

_____. *Harold Town Drawings*. Toronto: McClelland and Stewart, 1969.

_____. "The Multiplicity of Harold Town." *artscanada*, April/May 1971, pp. 49-56.

_____. "Introduction" in *Poets and Other People. Drawings by Harold Town*. Windsor: Art Gallery of Windsor, 1980.

Hale, Barrie. "Introduction." In *Toronto Painting: 1953-1965*. Ottawa: National Gallery of Canada, 1972.

_____. "Out of the Park. Modernist Painting in Toronto, 1950-1980." *Provincial Essays*, Vol. 2. Toronto: Phacops Publishing Society, 1985.

Harold Town. The First Exhibition of New Work. 1969-1973. Oshawa: The Robert McLaughlin Gallery, 1973.

Hawkes, Donald. "It's magic, nostalgia, scruffy movie houses - and joy too." *The Globe and Mail*, 13 November 1971.

Heine, William. "Points of View Make a Lively Show." *Weekend Magazine*, vol. 8, no. 45 (1958), pp. 6, 17.

Heywood, Irene. "Town's latest challenge: heroes and hippies." *The Gazette* (Montreal), 23 May 1970.

Jasmin, Claude. "Un western pictural avec Town." *La Presse* (Montreal), 16 December 1961.

_____. "The Art Scene." *Toronto Star*, 21 April 1962.

_____. "Painter-Sculptors." *Canadian Art*, July/August 1962.

_____. "Academy's 1964 exhibition traditional and successful." *Toronto Star*, 25 January 1964.

_____. *Great Canadian Painting: A Century of Art*. Toronto: The Canadian Centennial Publishing Co. Ltd., 1966.

Kirkman, Terry, and Herviz, Judy. "Town Exhibition Rich in Diversity." *The Montreal Star*, 17 March 1972.

Kritzwiser, Kay. "Harold Town is Back in Town." *The Globe and Mail*, 29 January 1966.

_____. "Harold goes to town with Enigmas." *The Globe and Mail*, 12 April 1969.

_____. "Ah what memories up there on the wall." *The Globe and Mail*, 8 November 1969.

_____. "Lights, ideas, action – it's Town power." *The Globe and Mail*, 5 December 1970.

_____. "Town: from innovation to proficiency short on heart." *The Globe and Mail*, 11 October 1975.

Levene, Constance. "Harold Town at the Andrew-Morris Gallery, New York City." *Canadian Art*, May/June 1963, pp. 147-48.

Lord, Barry. *The History of Painting in Canada: Towards a People's Art*. Toronto: NC Press, 1974.

MacCarthy, Pearl. "To disagree harmoniously - object of 'Painters Eleven'." *The Globe and Mail*, 13 February 1954.

_____. "OSA shows Canadian Art Strong." *The Globe and Mail*, March 1957.

_____. "Town and his country: the realm of power and the river." *The Globe Magazine*, 25 October 1958.

_____. "Town Show a Mixed Stimulant." *The Globe and Mail*, 4 March 1961, p. 15.

Malcolmson, Harry. "Where have all the artists gone?" *The Toronto Telegram*, 21 August 1965.

_____. "Introduction." *Paintings 1964; Paintings 1965*. Toronto : Mazelow Gallery and Jerrold Morris International Gallery, 1966.

_____. "Art and Artists," *The Toronto Telegram*, 5 February 1966.

Mays, John Bentley. " 'Garage Sale' good for a laugh," *The Globe and Mail*, 16 May 1981.

Moon, Barbara. "The Overnight Bull Market in Modern Art." *Maclean's*, 2 December 1961, pp.222-23.

Morris, Jerrold. *Harold Town: 1954/1959; Prints and Collages*. Toronto, 1967.

Murray, Joan. *Painters Eleven in Retrospect*. Oshawa: The Robert McLaughlin Gallery, 1971.

_____. "Galleries. Himself Surprised." *Toronto Calendar*, June 1981.

Phillips, Alan. "Canadian Painting's Angriest Young Man." *Star Weekly*, 2 April 1960.

de Repentigny, Rodolphe. "Le Groupe des Onze." *Vie des Arts*, automne 1958, pp. 27-33.

_____. "Deux excellents peintres Canadiens." *La Presse*, March 1957.

Russell, Paul. "Artist Harold Town through Three Styles." *Toronto Star*, 5 December 1970.

Silcox, David P. "Harold Town at The Jerrold Morris Gallery, Toronto," *Canadian Art*, July/August 1962, pp. 259-60.

_____. "Canadian Art in the Sixties." *Canadian Art*, January 1966, pp. 55-61.

_____. "Introduction." *Harold Town. The First Exhibition of New Work, 1969-1973*. Oshawa: The Robert McLaughlin Gallery, 1973.

Tovell, Vincent. "Eleven Painters Start a War." *Canadian Commentator*, November 1957.

Anon. "Toronto School-Kids exposed to Filthy Painting." *Flash*, 22 December 1951.

Unknown. "Canada's Angriest Young Man, The Art and Wrath of Harold Town." *The Chicago Tribune*, 5 February 1967, p. 34.

Anon. "Around the Galleries." *Time Magazine*, 16 October 1964.

Withrow, William J. *Contemporary Canadian Painting*. Toronto: McClelland & Stewart, 1972.

CATALOGUE OF THE EXHIBITION

ABBREVIATIONS

Exhibitions in italics refer to one-man shows.

AEAC   Agnes Etherington Art Centre
AFA   American Federation of the Arts
CGP   Canadian Group of Painters
CNE   Canadian National Exhibition
GCA   Gallery of Canadian Art
KWAG   Kitchener-Waterloo Art Gallery
LRAG   London Regional Art Gallery
MOMA   Museum of Modern Art
P11   Painters Eleven
PLS   Picture Loan Society
RMG   The Robert McLaughlin Gallery
VAG   Vancouver Art Gallery

PAINTINGS

Sancho, Don Quixote and Rocinante
1949-50
Oil on masonite
121.9 x 38.7 cm
Exhibited: 1951 OSA; 1951 CNE; 1953
Robertson; 1975 *Windsor*
The Artist

Side Show Performer 1950
Oil on masonite
Inscribed: (l.l.) *Town Jy 50*
Exhibited: 1951 CNE
The Artist

Three Musicians 1949-50
Oil on masonite
120 x 134.3 cm
Not previously exhibited
The Artist

Two Nudes 1951
Oil on masonite
122.6 x 76.8 cm
Exhibited: 1951 RCA; 1975 *Windsor*
The Artist

The Window in the Studio 1952
Oil on masonite
130.1 x 78.7 cm
Inscribed: (u.l.) *Town 7-6-52*
Exhibited: 1975 *Windsor*
The Artist

Conversation between Clowns 1953
Oil on masonite
74.9 x 121.3 cm
Inscribed: (l.l.) *Town Nov 53*
Exhibited: 1954 Roberts, Robertson; 1975
Windsor
The Artist

Essence of Rex 1953
Oil on masonite
101.0 x 73.0 cm
Inscribed: (l.l.) *Town 53*
Exhibited: 1954 Roberts, Robertson;
1979 RMG
The Artist

Mechanical Forest Sound 1953
Oil on masonite
121.9 x 170.2 cm
Exhibited: 1955 OSA
The Artist

Morning Alarm 1953-54
Oil on masonite
110.5 x 121.9 cm
Exhibited: 1954 CGP
The Artist

Through Forest the Jungle of Industry c. 1954
Oil on masonite
176.8 x 104.8 cm
Inscribed: (l.r.) *Town 56* [inscribed later]
Not previously exhibited
The Artist

Bagatelle 1954
Oil and collage on masonite
Inscribed: (u.l.) *Town 54-3-7*
Exhibited: 1957 *GCA*
Collection of Mr. & Mrs. L. Trevor RCA

Neons at Noon 1954
Oil on masonite
121.9 x 121.9 cm
Inscribed: (l.l.) *Town 54*
Exhibited: 1955 Roberts, YWCA;
1955 Winnipeg
The Artist

In Kite White 1955-56
Oil on masonite
121.9 x 109.9 cm
Inscribed:
Not previously exhibited
The Artist

Fall of Babylon 1956
Oil and lucite on canvas
223.5 x 67.9 cm
Inscribed: (u.r.) *Town 56*
Exhibited: 1956 CNE
The Artist

The Dixon Passing Mugg's Island 1956
Oil on masonite
121.9 x 124.5 cm
Inscribed: (l.r.) *Town 4-2-56*
Exhibited: 1957 GCA; 1972 NGC, AGO;
1960 *Regina*
The Artist

Monument to a Politician 1956
Oil and lucite on canvas
243.8 x 97.8 cm
Inscribed: (u.l.) *Town 56*
Exhibited: 1957 GCA; 1957 Sao Paulo;
1975 *Windsor*
Collection of the Sarnia Public Library and
Art Gallery

Monument 1957
Oil and lucite on canvas
214.6 x 165.1 cm
Exhibited: 1960 OSA
The Artist

Variation on a Variation 1957
Oil and lucite on masonite
121.9 x 121.9 cm
Inscribed: (l.r.) *Town 57*
Exhibited: 1957 Park
Collection of Mrs. O.D. Vaughan

Landscape with Reed 1957
Oil and lucite on canvas
121.9 x 121.9 cm
Exhibited: 1958 *Tooth*; 1961 *Laing*
Inscribed: (l.l.) *Town 57*
Anonymous Loan

The Turner Reprise 1958-60
Oil and lucite on masonite
121.9 x 167.6 cm
Inscribed: (l.r.) *Town 58-60*
Exhibited: 1975 *Windsor*
The Art Gallery of Windsor

Untitled 1959-60
Oil and lucite on canvas
204.0 x 275.0 cm
Inscribed:
On loan from the Canada Council Art Bank/
Pret de la Banque d'oeuvres d'art du Conseil
des Arts du Canada

Harvest 1960
Oil and lucite on masonite
91.4 x 61.0 cm
Inscribed: (u.l.) Town 60
Exhibited: 1961 *Laing*; 1961 Sao Paulo; 1975
Windsor
Collection of Jessica & Percy Waxer

For Corbu 1960
Oil and lucite on canvas
205.7 x 188.0 cm
Inscribed: (l.r.) *Town 1960*
Not previously exhibited
The Artist

Pitch Out 1960
Oil and lucite on canvas
200.7 x 172.7 cm
Inscribed: (l.r. incised) Town 60
Exhibited: 1961 *Laing*; 1967 *Douglas*;
1975 Windsor
The Artist

Interior Pitch Out 1960
Oil and lucite on canvas
173.4 x 198.8 cm
Not previously exhibited
The Artist

Inoutscape 1960
Oil and lucite on Belgian linen
206.4 x 189.2 cm
Inscribed: (l.l.) *Town 1960*
Not previously exhibited
The Artist

Enter the Empress 1960
Oil and lucite on canvas
208.3 x 172.7 cm
Inscribed: (l.r.) *Town 60*
Exhibited: 1961 *Laing*
Art Gallery of Ontario, Gift from the McLean
Foundation, 1961

Target No. 2 1960
Oil and lucite on canvas
202.6 x 174.0 cm
Inscribed: (incised u.r.) *Town 60*
Exhibited: 1961 *Laing*
The Artist

Banners 1960
Oil and lucite on canvas
183.5 x 182.9 cm
Exhibited: 1961 *Laing*; 1964 NGC; 1964
Venice; 1966 VAG; 1975 *Windsor*; 1981 KWAG
Norman MacKenzie Art Gallery, Regina

Juggling in Rousseau's Dark 1960
Oil and lucite on canvas
208.3 x 173.0 cm
Inscribed: (c.r.) *Town 60*
Exhibited: 1961 *Laing*
The Artist

Wright Flight (Memorial) 1961
Oil and lucite on canvas
205.7 x 188.0 cm
Inscribed: (l.r.) *Town 61*
Exhibited: 1970 *Waddington; Mazelow;*
1962 *Morris*
The Artist

Great Seal No. 1 1961
Oil and lucite on canvas
186.7 x 209.6 cm
Inscribed: (u.r.) *Town -61-*
Exhibited: 1962 *Morris*; 1962 *Andrew-Morris;*
1964 *Vancouver*
Art Gallery of Ontario. Purchase,
Corporations' Subscription Endowment 1962

Down and Up 1961
Oil and lucite on canvas
172.7 x 198.1 cm
Not previously exhibited
The Artist

Cool One 1961
Oil and lucite on canvas
152.4 x 205.7 cm
Not previously exhibited
The Artist

Armoured Explorer 1961
Oil and lucite on canvas
188.0 x 205.7 cm
Inscribed: (c.l.) *Town 61*
Exhibited: 1962 *Morris*
The Artist

A Child's Christmas in Toronto 1961
Oil and lucite on canvas
152.4 x 213.4 cm
Exhibited: 1962 *Morris*; 1966 *Waddington*
Montreal Museum of Fine Arts. Gift of Dr.
Sean Murphy.

Empty Burden 1961
Oil and lucite on canvas
188.6 x 206.4 cm
Inscribed: (l.r.) *Town 61*
Exhibited: 1962 *Morris*; 1963 MOMA
The Artist

Festival 1961
Oil and lucite on canvas
206.0 x 188.5 cm
On loan from the Canada Council Art
Bank/Pret de la Banque d'oeuvres d'art du
Conseil des Arts du Canada

Oracle Set 1961
Oil and lucite on canvas
182.9 x 213.4 cm
Inscribed: (l.r.) *Town 61*
Exhibited: 1962 *Morris*
Collection of Sam & Esther Sarick

Pursuit Set 1962
Oil and lucite on canvas
213.4 x 152.4 cm
The Artist

Uncas Set No. 2 1962
Oil and lucite on canvas
206.1 x 152.7 cm
Exhibited: 1963 Guggenheim; 1964 Tate
Collection of the Solomon R. Guggenheim
Museum, New York

Copernicus Set 1962
Oil and lucite on canvas
205.7 x 190.5 cm
Exhibited: 1964 Kassel; 1975 *Windsor*
The Artist

Parkin Set 1962
Oil and lucite on canvas
205.7 x 152.4 cm
Inscribed: (u.c.r.) *Town 62*
Exhibited: 1964 *Venice*
The Artist

Sunday Painter's Set 1962
Oil and lucite on canvas
205.6 x 153.6 cm
Inscribed: (l.r.) *Town 62*
Exhibited: 1966 *Morris*
London Regional Art Gallery, Gift of the
Volunteer Committee, 1966

Card Set 1962
Oil and lucite on canvas
207.2 x 162.6 cm
Inscribed: (l.r.) *Town 62*
Exhibited: 1963 Madrid
Private Collection

Tyranny of the Corner. Judge Set 1962
Oil and lucite on canvas
188.6 x 206.4 cm
Inscribed: (l.c.r.) *Town 62*
Exhibited: 1966 *Morris*; 1966 *Waddington*
Collection of Montreal Museum of Fine Arts.
Gift of David Y. Hodgson, 1976

Tyranny of the Corner, Cliffhanger 1962
Oil and lucite on canvas
205.7 x 162.6 cm
The Artist

Entrance of the Tyranny of the Corner 1962
Oil and lucite on canvas
206.4 x 163.2 cm
Inscribed: (u.r.) *Town 62*
Exhibited: 1963 RCA
The Artist

Tyranny of the Corner 1962
Oil and lucite on canvas
206.5 x 164.0 cm
On loan from the Canada Council Art
Bank/Pret de la Banque d'oeuvres d'art du
Conseil des Arts du Canada

Mondrian Inscape Set 1962
Oil and lucite on canvas
152.4 x 213.4 cm
Inscribed: (l.r.) *Town 62*
The Artist

Traffic Set 1963
Oil and lucite on canvas
188.0 x 206.0 cm
Inscribed: (u.r.) *Town 63*
Collection of Sam & Esther Sarick

Parade Set 1963
Oil and lucite on canvas
203.2 x 152.4 cm
Inscribed: (l.r.) *Town 63*
Exhibited: 1964 Vancouver
Collection of Dr. & Mrs. Sydney L. Wax

Tyranny of the Corner 1963
Oil and lucite on canvas
188.0 x 205.7 cm
Inscribed: (l.l.) *Town 63*
On loan from The Imperial Life Assurance
Company of Canada

Helicopter 1963
Oil and lucite on canvas
188.0 x 205.7 cm
Inscribed: (u.r.) *Town 63*
The Artist

In Memory of Pearl McCarthy 1964
Oil and lucite on canvas
205.7 x 188.0 cm
Inscribed: (l.r.) *Town 64*
Exhibited: 1966 *Morris*; 1966 *Mazelow*
Collection of Mr. & Mrs. W.B. Herman

Optical 1964
Oil and lucite on canvas
203.2 x 208.1 cm
Inscribed: (l.r.) *Town 64*
Collection of AGF Management Limited

Optical No. 9 1964
Oil and lucite on canvas
152.5 x 152.5 cm
Museum of Modern Art, New York

No-Op No. 2 1964
Oil and lucite on canvas
206.0 x 163.0 cm
Exhibited: 1966 *Mazelow*
On loan from the Canada Council Art
Bank/Pret de la Banque d'oeuvres d'art du
Conseil des Arts du Canada

No-Op No. 3 1964
Oil and lucite on canvas
206.5 x 162.3 cm
Inscribed: (l.r.) *Town 64*
Exhibited: 1964 New York
Art Gallery of Hamilton. Gift of Marcia
Klamer, 1979

The Great Divide 1965
Oil and lucite on canvas
228.6 x 152.4 cm
Inscribed: (l.l.) *Town 65*; (l.r. incised) *Town 65*
Exhibited: 1966 *Morris*
Art Gallery of Ontario, Purchase, 1966

Glory Hole 1965
Oil and lucite on canvas
205.7 x 162.6 cm
Inscribed: (l.r. incised) *Town 65*
Exhibited: 1966 *Morris*
Collection of National Gallery of Canada,
Ottawa

Centrebiz 1965
Oil and lucite on canvas
132.1 x 133.4 cm
Inscribed: (l.r.) *Town 65*
Exhibited: 1966 *Morris*
London Regional Art Gallery, General
Purchase Fund

Fate Curtain 1966
Oil and lucite on canvas
205.7 x 188.0 cm
Inscribed: (u.r.) *Town 66*
Exhibited: 1967 Chicago; 1967 Winnipeg;
1967 Ontario Pavilion; 1968 Edinburgh; 1970
Osaka; 1975 *Windsor*
The Art Gallery of Windsor. On permanent
loan from CKEY radio, Toronto, 1975.

Dot 1966
Oil and lucite on canvas
142.2 x 142.2 cm
Inscribed: (l.r.) *Town 66*
Exhibited: 1975 *Windsor*
Collection of Sam & Esther Sarick

Silent Light No. 15
Oil and lucite on canvas
60.0 x 91.4 cm
Exhibited: 1970 *Mazelow*
The Artist

Silent Light No. 11 1968-69
Oil and lucite on canvas
132.1 x 132.1 cm
Exhibited: 1970 *Mazelow*; 1975 *Windsor*
The Artist

Silent Light No. 21 1968-69-70
Oil and lucite on canvas
66.0 x 91.4 cm
Exhibited: 1970 *Mazelow*; 1975 *Windsor*
The Artist

Silent Light No. 30
Oil and lucite on canvas
66.0 x 91.4 cm
Exhibited: 1970 *Mazelow*
The Artist

Park No. 1 1970
Oil and lucite on canvas
185.5 x 187.5 cm
Exhibited: 1970 *Mazelow*; 1972 *Waddington*;
1973 *RMG*; 1975 *Windsor*
On loan from the Canada Council Art
Bank/Pret de la Banque d'oeuvres d'art du
Conseil des Arts du Canada

Park No. 5 1971
Oil and lucite on canvas
121.9 x 147.5 cm
Inscribed: (l.r.) *Town. 71.*
The Artist

Park No. 17 1971-72
Oil and lucite on canvas
121.9 x 121.9 cm
The Artist

Park No. 9 1972
Oil and lucite on canvas
152.4 x 152.4 cm
Inscribed: (l.r.) *Town 72*
Exhibited: 1975 *Windsor*
The Artist

Park No. 6 1972
Oil and lucite on canvas
177.8 x 177.8 cm
The Artist

Stretch No. 3 1968
Oil and lucite on canvas
152.4 x 228.6 cm
Inscribed: (l.r.) *Town 68*
Exhibited: 1970 *Mazelow*
The Artist

Stretch 1969
Oil and lucite on canvas
121.9 x 121.9 cm
Inscribed:
Exhibited: 1970 *Mazelow;* 1973 *RMG*
The Artist

Stretch No. 4 1969
Oil and lucite on canvas
161.3 x 161.3 cm
Inscribed: (l.r.) *Town 69*
Exhibited: *Mazelow* 1970
The Artist

Stretch No. 23 1970
Oil and lucite on canvas
274.5 x 96.7 cm
Inscribed: (l.r.) *Town 70*
Exhibited: 1970 *Mazelow;* 1972 *Waddington;*
1975 *Windsor*
The Artist

Stretch No. 27 1970
Oil and lucite on canvas
208.3 x 188.0 cm
Exhibited: 1970 *Mazelow;* 1972 *Waddington;*
1975 *Windsor*
The Artist

Stretch No. 30 1970
Oil and lucite on canvas
121.9 x 121.9 cm
Exhibited: 1970 *Mazelow*
The Artist

Snap No. 2 1972
Oil and lucite on canvas
172.7 x 172.7 cm
The Artist

Snap No. 36A 1973
Oil and lucite on canvas
205.7 x 188.0 cm
The Artist

Snap No. 49 1973
Oil and lucite on canvas
152.4 x 152.4 cm
Exhibited: 1973 *RMG;* 1973-74 *Mazelow*
The Artist

Snap No. 54 1973
Oil and lucite on canvas
152.4 x 228.6 cm
Exhibited: 1973-74 *Mazelow*
The Artist

Snap No. 66 1973-74
Oil and lucite on canvas
183.9 x 183.9 cm
Not previously exhibited
The Artist

Snap No. 80 1974
Oil and lucite on canvas
182.9 x 182.9 cm
Exhibited: 1975 *Mazelow*
The Artist

In Memory of Emelio del Junco 1974-75
Oil and lucite on canvas
188.0 x 228.6 cm
Inscribed: (incised l.l.) *Town 74-75*
Exhibited: 1975 *Windsor*
The Artist

Snap 1975
Oil and lucite on canvas
203.2 x 188.0 cm
Inscribed: (incised l.l.) *Town;* (l.r.) *Town 75*
Not previously exhibited
The Artist

Snap No. 86 1975
Oil and lucite on canvas
182.9 x 182.9 cm
Inscribed: (l.l. incised) *Town 75*
Exhibited: 1975 *Mazelow*
Art Gallery of Hamilton, gift of *The Hamilton
Spectator,* 1985

Snap No. 79 1975
Oil and lucite on canvas
188.0 x 254.0 cm
Exhibited: 1975 *Mazelow;* 1975 *Queen's Park*
Private collection, Toronto

Snap 1975
Oil and lucite on canvas
274.3 x 152.4 cm
Inscribed: (l.r. incised) *Town 75*
Not previously exhibited
The Artist

Snap 1976
Oil and lucite on canvas
182.9 x 182.9
Not previously exhibited
The Artist

*The Shade of Albert Franck returns disguised
as Rembrandt to fan the platitudes of
Post-Painterly Abstraction drying on the
Greenberg line* 1979-80
Oil on Belgian linen
183.0 x 183.0 cm
Inscribed: (l.r.) *Town 79-80*
Exhibited: 1981 *Waddington*
The Artist

*Charles Waterton (1782-1865) attempts to cure
his sprained ankle in the "tremendous
cascade" of Niagara Falls* 1980
Oil and lucite on canvas
304.8 x 152.4 cm
Not previously exhibited
The Artist

*Charles K. Ogden changes the underdrawers
on the mummified body of the English
philosopher Jeremy Bentham* 1980-81
Oil and lucite on canvas
304.8 x 152.4 cm
Exhibited: 1981 *Waddington*
The Artist

*Spengler writing "The Decline of the West" at
his desk on top of the kitchen table* 1980
Oil and lucite on canvas
228.6 x 188.0 cm
Exhibited: 1981 *Waddington*
Collection of Sam & Esther Sarick

*Art Establishment changes from Matisse to
Picasso Time* 1980
Oil and lucite on canvas
188.0 x 228.6 cm
Inscribed: (u.l.) *Town 80*
Exhibited: 1981 *Waddington*
Collection of Garth H. Drabinsky

*Snowy Farr, The Demon Sweep of
Cambridgeshire* 1980-81
Oil and lucite on canvas
188.6 x 230.0 cm
Exhibited: 1981 *Waddington*
The Artist

*Where do the bums go when they leave their
pants in the Rosedale Valley ravine?* 1980
Oil and lucite on canvas
229.2 x 188.6 cm
Inscribed: (u.l.) *Town 80*
Exhibited: 1981 *Waddington*
The Artist

*Painting for Beatrice White - Winner of the
1912 Toronto Fly Killing Contest with a Score
of 543,360 dead insects* 1980
Oil and lucite on canvas
230.0 x 188.6 cm
Inscribed: (c.r.) *Town 80*
Exhibited: 1981 *Waddington*
The Artist

Musclemen No. 3 1981
Oil and lucite on canvas
152.4 x 304.9 cm
Exhibited: 1985 AEAC
The Artist

Muscleman 1983
Oil and lucite on canvas
71.1 x 81.3 cm
Not previously exhibited
The Artist

Musclemen 1983
Oil and lucite on canvas
121.9 x 152.4 cm
Inscribed: (l.r.) *Town Feb 83.*
Not previously exhibited
The Artist

Muscleman 1983
Oil and lucite on canvas
121.9 x 137.2 cm
Not previously exhibited
The Artist

Muscleman 1984
Oil and lucite on canvas
101.6 x 78.7 cm
Inscribed: (l.r.) *Town 84.*
Not previously exhibited
The Artist

Musclemen 1984
Oil and lucite on canvas
137.2 x 167.6 cm
Not previously exhibited
The Artist

COLLAGES

In Air Above the Poet's House 1956
Collage
243.8 x 121.9 cm
Inscribed: (l.r.) *Town 56*
Exhibited: 1959 OSA; 1959 Stratford; 1960
Montreal, P11; 1960 *Regina;* 1963 MOMA;
1975 *Windsor*
Private collection, Toronto

Dream of the Samurai 1957
Collage (Single autographic print fragments,
tissue paper, ink, tube paint)
121.9 x 121.9 cm
Inscribed: (l.r.) *Town 11-11-57*
Not previously exhibited
The Artist

First Spring 1957
Collage
99.0 x 99.0 cm
Inscribed: (u.r.) *Town 4.57*
Exhibited: 1961 *Laing*
Collection of Mr. & Mrs. H. Klamer, Toronto

Monument to C. T. Currelly No. 1 1957
Collage
121.9 x 121.9 cm
Inscribed: (l.r.) *Town 16-7-57*
Exhibited: 1958 Vancouver, CGP; 1975
Windsor
Collection of Vancouver Art Gallery

July 1957
Collage (Single autographic print fragments,
tissue paper, wrapping paper, wax resist, pen
and ink)
182.9 x 121.9 cm
Inscribed: (u.l.) *Town 58* [changed from 57 to
58]
Not previously exhibited
Collection of Dr. & Mrs. Sydney L. Wax

Garden for Eurasian Princess 1957-58
Collage (Single autographic print fragments,
tissue paper, ink, gouache)
182.9 x 121.9 cm
Inscribed: (l.l.) *Town 58* [changed from 57 to
58]
Exhibited: 1959 CGP; 1961 *Dresdnere*
Collection of Joan & Martin Goldfarb

Garden of Nebuchadnezzar 1958
Collage and mixed media on masonite
121.9 x 119.4 cm
Inscribed: (u.r.) *Town 58*
Exhibited: 1959 *Jordan;* 1959 NGC; 1968
Mont-Royal
Collection of Montreal Museum of Fine Arts

Odd Wheel Out 1958
Collage (fluorescent tube packing, wood
sub-lining from mirror, tube oil paint, silk
stocking, tissue paper and various wrapping
materials on plywood)
143.5 x 121.9 cm
Inscribed: (u.l.) *Town 1958*
Not previously exhibited
The Artist

Music Behind 1958-59
Collage
121.9 x 121.9 cm
Inscribed: (l.r.) *Town 58-59*
Exhibited: 1972 NGC, AGO; 1967 *Morris*
Collection of National Gallery of Canada, Ottawa

Hokusai See-Through 1958-60
Collage (egg carton, antique linen, burned
and painted from back, gouache, wood
construction, basket handle on untempered
masonite)
243.8 x 121.9 cm
Inscribed: (l.r.) *Town 58/59/60*
Not previously exhibited
The Artist

Screen 1959-60-61
Collage (dry-sack bag with oil paint, hesian,
shingle, pegboard, drywall, antique linen,
scratching from cat "Moby," unfinished
unprinted woodblock, hesian, linen, lace
doily, matt board, burning, plywood,
wallpaper samples, fabric remnants on four
panels painting crate joined with piano
hinges)
243.5 x 50.4 cm (each panel); 243.5 x 201.8
cm overall
Inscribed: (l.l. first panel, front) *Town 59.60;*
(c.l. first panel, back) *Town 60/61;* (c.r. third
panel, back) *Town 59-60-61*
Exhibited: 1979 AEAC
The Artist

Architectural Trial 1960-61
Collage (plywood crate top from VAG, 4
panels, hydro-cal over hesian with burnt
plastic containers, corrugated paper,
fluorescent light paking material, paint skin,
pencil shavings, tissue paper, egg carton, silk
stocking, wicker basket, golf ball, metal bottle
cap)
153.0 x 134.6 cm
Inscribed: (u.r.) *Town 60/61;* (l.l. inverted)
Town 60/61
Not previously exhibited
The Artist

Untitled 1960
Collage on masonite
121.9 x 121.9 cm
Inscribed: (l.r.) *Town 60*
Exhibited: 1961 *Laing;* 1962 *Morris*
The Artist

Presence with Predecessor 1960
Collage with acrylic
121.9 x 121.9 cm
Inscribed: (l.r.) *Town 11-5-60*
Exhibited: 1961 OSA
Art Gallery of Windsor Collection. Gift of
Pierre Berton, Toronto, 1979

Entrance of the Stage Left Dragon 1960
Collage (Tissue paper, tube paint, gold foil,
single autographic print fragments, gouache,
wrapping paper)
121.9 x 91.4 cm
Inscribed: (u.l.) *Town-1960*
Exhibited: 1961 *Laing*
Collection of Sam & Esther Sarick

Departure 1960
Open weave hesian, antique linen, gouache
with pastel scumbled over
160.0 x 121.9 cm
Inscribed: (c.r.) *Town 60*
Exhibited: 1961 *Laing;* 1979 AEAC
The Artist

The Abstract Expressionist Kid's Punch Out
1960-61-62
Collage (Punch-out material from children's
books, Single autographic prints, gouache, ink
tissue paper, on 3/8" plywood)
100.0 x 122.0 cm
Inscribed: (l.r.) *Town 60/61/62*
Not previously exhibited
The Artist

Sculpture Pond 1960-61
Collage (Antique shea's linen drawn back and
front, linen remnants over wood cut with jig
saw)
121.9 x 144.9 cm
Inscribed: (u.l.) *Town 60/61*
Not previously exhibited
The Artist

Epiphany 1960-61
Antique linen, tissue paper, hydro-cal All,
gouache, pastel, burning
121.9 x 144.8 cm
Inscribed: (u.l.) *Town 60-61*
Not previously exhibited
The Artist

The Abstract Expressionist Kid's Punch Out
1960-61-62
Collage (Punch-out material from children's
books, Single autographic prints, gouache, ink
tissue paper, on 3/8" plywood)
100.0 x 122.0 cm
Inscribed: (l.r.) *Town 60/61/62*
Not previously exhibited
The Artist

Death of Mondrian No. 1 1961
Collage
121.3 x 118.7 cm
Inscribed: (l.r.) *Town 61*
Exhibited: 1962 Louisville; 1962 Warsaw;
1964 *Venice*; 1967 London; 1975 *Windsor*;
1976 LRAG
London Regional Art Gallery on permanent
loan from the Ontario Heritage Foundation,
gift of Mr. T.H. Moore

Yesterday, Today and Tomorrow 1940-1985
Computer parts, canvas, baseball, plaster cast,
chains, British mortar carrier, computer
cable, rubber hose on plywood faced doors
211.5 x 274.8 x 36.2 cm (irregular)
Not previously exhibited
The Artist

All Symbols are Signs All Signs are Symbols
1967-1985
Brass rubbing by W. de Courcy Prideaux (Oct.
1911); splash guards and paper graphs on
masonite
446.0 x 223.0 cm
Inscribed: (l.r.) *Town 1967-1985*
Not previously exhibited
The Artist

Mondrian and Pollock Memorial No. 3
1975-85
Tape (from Silent Lights paintings),
cardboard, acrylic, pencil on two doors
228.6 x 200.4 cm
Inscribed: *Town 75-85*
Not previously exhibited
The Artist

Modern Times Print Out 1981-85
Trial package proofs, annual report graphs,
acid free board on masonite door
230.0 x 71.1 cm
Inscribed: (l.l.) *Town 81-85*
Not previously exhibited
The Artist

Canadian Retirement Dream 1982-85
Oil paint, annual report graphs, plastic, paper
on masonite
245.0 x 121.9 cm
Inscribed: (u.r.) *Town 83-85*
Not previously exhibited
The Artist

The Weather Report (A Paean to Inaccuracy)
1984-85
Mixed media collage on door
332.5 x 193.0 cm (irregular)
Not previously exhibited
The Artist

Time Centre 1984-85
Acrylic, protractors and temperature control
graphs, plastic and bamboo on masonite
243.8 x 121.9 cm
Inscribed: *Town 84-85*
Not previously exhibited
The Artist

Tomorrow Doorway 1985
Warped door with one side of masonite
surface removed
225.4 x 121.9 x 91.4 cm
Not previously exhibited
The Artist

Space Shingles 1985
Card with tape (from Snap paintings) and oil
203.2 x 71.1 cm
Not previously exhibited
The Artist

SINGLE AUTOGRAPHIC PRINTS

Sizes refer to the plate size. All inscriptions
are outside the plate.

Up and Down 1954
Single autographic print
50.2 x 40.3 cm
Inscribed: (l.l.) *1.-1.*; (l.r.) *Town 1954*
Exhibited: 1967 De Cordova
The Artist

Boadicea's Arch 1956
Single autographic print
50.2 x 40.3 cm
Inscribed: (l.r.) *Town 56*
Exhibited: 1967 De Cordova
The Artist

The Latch 1956
Single autographic print
50.2 x 40.3 cm
Inscribed: (l.l.) *Town 1956;* (l.r.) *1-1*
Collection of University of Lethbridge Art
Gallery

Bromius Bop 1956
Single autographic print
50.2 x 40.3 cm
Inscribed: (l.l.) *1-1;* (l.r.) *Town 56*
Collection of University of Lethbridge Art
Gallery

The Aura of Yang-Kue-Fei 1956
Single autographic print
40.3 x 50.2 cm
Inscribed: (l.l.) *Town 56;* (l.r.) *1-1*
Exhibited: 1956 AGT; 1956 Venice; 1958
Utrecht; 1975 *Windsor*
Art Gallery of Windsor Collection. Gift of
Artist, 1985

Pyre of Celestial Parts 1956
Single autographic print and collage
50.2 x 40.3 cm
Inscribed: (l.r.) *Town 56*
Exhibited: 1956 *PLS*
The Artist

Departure of the Alphabet 1957
Single autographic print
40.3 x 50.2 cm
Inscribed: (l.l.) *1-1;* (l.r.) *Town 57*
Exhibited: 1956 *PLS;* 1964 *Venice;* 1967 Hart
House; 1967 Burnaby; 1975 *Windsor*
The Artist

The Place of the Samurai 1957
Single autographic print
50.2 x 40.3 cm
Inscribed: (l.r.) *Town 5./1.57*
Exhibited: 1964 *Venice*
The Artist

Winter Tree
Single autographic print
50.2 x 40.3 cm
Inscribed: (l.l.) *1./1.-;* (l.r.) *Town 62-* (inscribed
later)
Exhibited: 1962 Tokyo; 1963 Santiago
Collection of Metropolitan Museum of Art,
New York

Radar Detecting Winter
Single autographic print
50.2 x 40.3 cm
Inscribed: (l.l.) *1-.2.;* (l.r.) *Town 62* (inscribed
later)
Exhibited: 1967 De Cordova
The Artist

The First Infernal Submarine 1957
Single autographic print
45.6 x 60.3 cm
Inscribed: (l.l.) *Town 1-12-57;* (l.r.) *1-1-*
Exhibited: 1960 *MMFA*
Collection of Museum of Modern Art, New
York. Advisory Committee Fund.

Focus 1957
Single autographic print and collage
50.2 x 40.3 cm
Inscribed: (l.l.) *1-1*; (l.r.) *Town 1957*
Exhibited: 1967 *Mazelow*
Private collection

The Ruins of Oceanus 1957
Single autographic print
40.3 x 50.2 cm
Inscribed: (l.r.) *Town 1-12/57*
Exhibited: 1957 Sao Paulo; 1964 *Venice;* 1967
De Cordova; 1975 *Windsor;*
The Artist

The Dissident 1957
Single autographic print
40.3 x 50.2 cm
Inscribed: (l.l.) *Town 57;* (l.r.) *1-1*
Exhibited: 1962 Tokyo
Mr. & Mrs. Jack Shadbolt, Burnaby, British
Columbia

Gateway to Atlantis No. 1 1957
Single autographic print
40.3 x 50.2 cm
Inscribed: (l.l.) *Town .57*
Exhibited: 1958 Jordan; 1965 Dorothy
Cameron, Printmaking
Collection of Dorothy Cameron-Bloore

Gateway to Atlantis No. 2 1957
Single autographic print
40.3 x 50.2 cm
Inscribed: (l.l.) *Town 57-3.11-*
Exhibited: 1957 Winnipeg; 1960 MMFA,
Annual; 1964 *Venice;* 1967 Burnaby; 1975
Windsor
The Artist

Festival of Lemuria 1957
Single autographic print and collage
50.2 x 40.3 cm
Inscribed: (l.r.) *Town 5/12/57*
Exhibited: 1959-60 AFA; 1967-68 NGC tour;
1979 AEAC
The Artist

The Big Bite 1957
Single autographic print
50.2 x 40.3 cm
Inscribed: (l.l.) *1-1*; (l.r.) *Town 57*
The Artist

Machine of Cagliostro 1957-58
Single autographic print and collage
40.3 x 50.2 cm
Inscribed: (l.r.) *Town 57-58*
Exhibited: 1964 *Venice;* 1967 De Cordova;
1975 *Windsor*
The Artist

The Meeting
Single autographic print
40.3 x 50.2 cm
Inscribed: (l.l.) *1-1*; (l.r.) *Town 62* (inscribed
later)
Exhibited: 1964 *Venice;* 1965 Dorothy
Cameron, Printmaking; 1967 De Cordova
The Artist

Memory of High Park 1957-58
Single autographic print
40.3 x 50.2 cm
Inscribed: (l.r.) *Town 57-58*
Exhibited: 1964 London
London Regional Art Gallery, General
Purchase Fund, 1958

The Curve at Clandeboye 1958
Single autographic print
40.3 x 50.2 cm
Inscribed: (l.l.) *Town 5.1.58*
Exhibited: 1958 Brussels; 1958 Dallas; 1964
Venice; 1969 Guelph; 1975 *Windsor*
The Artist

Seaburst 1958
Single autographic print
40.3 x 50.2 cm
Inscribed: (l.r.) *Town 2-28.58* (57 changed to
58)
Exhibited: 1959 Ljubljana; 1964 *Venice;* 1965
Dorothy Cameron, Printmaking; 1967
Burnaby; 1975 *Windsor*
The Artist

Monument to an Unpublished Poet 1958
Single autographic print and collage
50.2 x 40.3 cm
Inscribed: (l.l.) *1-1*; (l.r.) *Town 58-*
Exhibited: 1962 MOMA; 1971 RMG
The Artist

Symbol for Poundmaker 1958
Single autographic print
50.2 x 40.3 cm
Inscribed: (l.l.) *1-1*; (l.r.) *Town 58*
The Artist

Totem for Tinker 1958
Single autographic print
50.2 x 40.3 cm
Inscribed: (l.l.) *Town 1-12.58*
Exhibited: 1967 De Cordova
The Artist

Radar Detecting Spring 1959
Single autographic print
45.7 x 61.0 cm
Inscribed: (l.l.) *1-1*; (l.r.) *Town 59*
Exhibited: 1960 Cincinnati
Collection of Museum of Modern Art, New
York, Elizabeth Bliss Parkinson Fund.

Signpost
Single autographic print
50.2 x 40.3 cm
Inscribed: (l.l.) *3-6;* (l.r.) *Town 60* (inscribed
later)
Exhibited: 1964 *Venice;* 1967 De Cordova
The Artist

WORKS ON PAPER

Enigma I 1964
Brush, steel pen, black and white inks on grey
green Fabriano
48.3 x 61.6 cm
Inscribed: (u.l.) *Town 12-13.1/64*
Exhibited: 1964 *Morris;* 1964 *Venice;* 1975
Windsor
The Artist

Enigma 29 1964
Brush, steel pen, black and white inks on
green paper
48.3 x 62.2 cm
Inscribed: (l.l.) *Town 23-6-2/7. 1964*
The Artist

Enigma 28 1964
Brush, steel pen, black and white inks on
green paper
48.3 x 62.2 cm
Inscribed: (l.r.) *Town 23/6 to 2/7-1964*
The Artist

Enigma No. 9 1964
Brush, steel pen, black and white inks on grey
paper
48.3 x 66.3 cm
Inscribed: (u.l.) *Town 2/2/64*
Exhibited: 1964 *Morris;* 1964 *Venice*
Mrs. W. Landauer

Enigma No. 10 1964
Brush, steel pen, black and white inks on
brown paper
48.4 x 57.5 cm
Inscribed: (u.l.) *Town 3-4-5-2/64*
Exhibited: 1964 *Morris;* 1964 *Venice*
Mrs. W. Landauer

Enigma 1964
Brush, steel pen, black and white inks on grey
paper
48.3 x 66.5 cm
Inscribed: (l.l.) *Town 16-17-18/64*
Exhibited: 1964 *Morris;* 1964 *Venice*
Mrs. W. Landauer

Enigma 38 1965
Brush, steel pen, black and white inks on grey
green paper
56.9 x 76.2 cm
Inscribed: (l.r.) *Town 10.3-20.4.65*
Exhibited: 1965 Dorothy Cameron, Eros; 1971
RMG; 1975 *Windsor*
The Artist

Enigma 1966
Brush, steel pen, black and white inks on grey
paper
55.7 x 76.2 cm
Inscribed: (l.l.) *Town 23-2 to 14-3/66*
The Artist

Enigma No. 42 1966
Brush, steel pen, black and white inks on gray
charcoal paper
55.9 x 76.2 cm
Inscribed: (l.r.) *Town 2/4 to 17/4.66-*
Exhibited: 1969 *Mazelow;* 1969 Windsor; 1975
Windsor
The Artist

Enigma 1967
Brush, steel pen, black and white inks on
brown paper
65.0 x 50.2 cm
Ins. (u.r.) Town 4-11 to 11-11 1967
The Artist

Enigma 1967-68
Brush, steel pen, black and white inks cork
print on brown paper
65.1 x 50.2 cm
Inscribed: (u.r.) *Town 27-12-67 to 9-2-1968*
Exhibited: 1969 *Mazelow;* 1969 *Windsor;* 1969
Bedford; 1975 *Windsor*
The Artist

Enigma 1968
Brush, steel pen, black and white inks on
brown paper
65.0 x 50.0 cm
Inscribed: (u.l.) *Town-1-10-to-25-10-1968-*
The Artist

Enigma 1968-69
Brush, steel pen, black and white inks on grey
50.2 x 65.0 cm
Inscribed: (u.l.) *Town 23.11-1968 to 20-1.69*
Exhibited: 1969 *Mazelow*
The Artist

Enigma 1972
Brush, steel pen, black and white inks on
brown paper
64.7 x 50.1 cm
Inscribed: (l.r.) *Town 30-6-10-24-7 1972*
The Artist

Enigma 1972
Brush, steel pen, black and white inks on
green paper
55.5 x 80.5 cm
Inscribed: (u.l.) *Town April-11 to 17 -1972*
The Artist

Lady in the Cook Photo 1969
Long brush, ink on salmon pink Ingres
Arches MBM paper
63.2 x 48.0 cm
Inscribed: (l.r.) *Town 15-6-69*
Not previously exhibited
The Artist

Lady in the Cook Photo 1970
Dry brush and ink on Montgolfier paper
65.3 x 50.1 cm
Inscribed: (l.r.) *Town 12-4-70*
Not previously exhibited
The Artist

Lady in the Cook Photo 1970
Conte on crescent board
76.4 x 43.8 cm
Inscribed: (l.r.) *Town 10-15/11/70*
Not previously exhibited
The Artist

Lady in the Cook Photo 1970
Graphite and eraser on crescent board
76.2 x 33.8 cm
Inscribed: (u.r.) *Town 15-11-70*
Not previously exhibited
The Artist

Lady in the Cook Photo 1970
Tracing wheel on crescent board
38.3 x 33.8 cm
Inscribed: (l.r.) *Town Nov 18-70*
Not previously exhibited
The Artist

Lady in the Cook Photo 1970
Ink concentrate, spray enamel, paper, brush
on crescent board
76.4 x 43.33 cm
Inscribed: (l.r.) *Town 2/18-11-70*
Not previously exhibited
The Artist

Lady in the Cook Photo 1970
Ink concentrate and glue on crescent board
2 parts; each 40.8 x 38.25 cm
Inscribed: (u.r. of right panel) *Town 70*
(scratched)
Not previously exhibited
The Artist

Lady in the Cook Photo 1971
Spray paint and tape on board
152.4 x 101.6 cm
Inscribed: (u.r.) *Town 10/11-1.71*
Exhibited: 1975 *Windsor*
The Artist

Lady in the Cook Photo 1971
Ink concentrate and brush on crescent board
38.1 x 38.3 cm
Inscribed: (l.r.) *Town 21-23-3 71*
Not previously exhibited
The Artist

Lady in the Cook Photo 1971
Steel pen and ink on crescent board
21.11 x 19.38 cm
Inscribed: (u.r.) *Town 28-30-3 71*
Not previously exhibited
The Artist

Lady in the Cook Photo 1971
Propane torch on crescent board
152.4 x 101.6 cm
Inscribed: (u.l.) *Town 5-4-71*
Exhibited: 1975 *Windsor*
The Artist

Lady in the Cook Photo 1971
Pen and ink, propane torch on crescent board
152.4 x 101.6 cm
Inscribed: (u.r.) *Town 5.11-6.71*
Not previously exhibited
The Artist

Lady in the Cook Photo 1971
Spray paint and tape, stencil and gouache on
crescent board
152.4 x 101.6 cm
Inscribed: (u.r.) *Town 71* (stencil)
Not previously exhibited
The Artist

Lady in the Cook Photo 1971
Conte on handmade paper
81 cm (uneven) x 59.4 cm
Inscribed: (l.r.) *Town 6-9-7-71*
Not previously exhibited
The Artist

Lady in the Cook Photo 1971
Compressed charcoal and eraser on Ingres
Arches MBM paper
64.8 x 50.0 cm
Inscribed: (l.r.) *Town 12-7-71*
Not previously exhibited
The Artist

Lady in the Cook Photo 1971
Charcoal, pastel and white pencil crayon on
Ingres Arches paper
65.1 x 50.1 cm
Inscribed: (u.r.) *Town 12-7-71*
Not previously exhibited
The Artist

Lady in the Cook Photo 1972
Ink wash on crescent board
24.1 x 20.3 cm
Inscribed: (u.r.) *Town 27-1-72*
Not previously exhibited
The Artist

Toy Horse 1976
Pencil, oil pastel, lead pencil, pastel pencil on
coloured paper
Inscribed: (u.r.) *Town Oct-14-76*
Not previously exhibited
The Artist

Toy Horse No. 132 1978
Pen, pencil, gouache and rubber stamp on
paper
56.0 x 76.0 cm
Mrs. S. Vaile

Toy Horse No. 230 1979
Brush, ink, mechanical pen, paint squiggle on paper
72.4 x 55.9 cm
Inscribed: (u.r.) *Town May 14-15.79*
Exhibited: 1984 *Moore*
Private collection, Scarborough

Toy Horse No. 134 1979
Gouache and watercolour on paper
55.9 x 75.2 cm
Inscribed: (u.l.) *Town Nov 79*
Not previously exhibited
Private collection, Toronto

Toy Horse No. 144 1980
Black ink and calligraphic pen on paper
72.4 x 57.2 cm
Inscribed: (u.l.) *Town June 25/80*
Exhibited: 1984 *Moore*
Anonymous Loan

Toy Horse No. 141 1980
Ink, coloured pencil, pen and wash on paper
50.8 x 69.9 cm
Inscribed: *Town Dec 10-15-80*
Exhibited: 1984 *Moore*
Mr. & Mrs. Pierre Berton

Toy Horse 1980-81
Pen, brush and ink, gouache, wash on MBM arches paper
62.3 x 47.6 cm
Inscribed: (u.l.) *Town Dec-23/80/Jan-5.81*
Not previously exhibited
The Artist

Toy Horse No. 192 1981
Collage, pen and ink, brush and ink, gouache, wax resist and watercolour on camber sand handmade paper
80.0 x 57.2 cm
Inscribed: (u.l.) *Town 18-19 Jan/81*
Exhibited: 1984 *Moore*
Collection of Mr. & Mrs. R. Campbell-Hain

Toy Horse No. 140 1981
Mechanical pen and ink, gouache and watercolour on paper
78.7 x 58.4 cm
Inscribed: (u.r.) *Town Feb 16-March 2.81*
Exhibited: 1984 *Moore*
Collection of H. Spencer Clark

Toy Horse No. 221 1982
Pen and ink, gouache, collage on paper
76.0 x 58.0 cm
Inscribed: (u.r.) *Town Jan-7-18.82*
Exhibited: 1984 *Moore*
Collection of Gloria Shulman

Toy Horse No. 256 1982
Acrylic and brush on crescent illustration board
151.8 x 101.6 cm
Inscribed: (u.r.) *Town Feb-28 March 2/82*
Exhibited: 1984 *Moore*
Collection of Karen & Raymond Oster

Toy Horse No. 270 1982
Pencil on paper
50.0 x 65.3 cm
Inscribed: (l.l.) *Town Oct-21/82*
Exhibited: 1984 *Moore*
Collection of H. Spencer Clark

Toy Horse No. 171 1982
Collage, gouache, mechanical pen and ink, steel pen
111.8 x 76.2 cm
Inscribed:
Exhibited: 1984 *Moore*
Collection of Fred L. G. Garner, Kitchener

Billie Dove 1927, "An Affair at the Follies" 1984
Pencil on acid free matt board
51.1 x 38.5 cm
Inscribed: (l.r.) *Town Oct 26/84*
Not previously exhibited
The Artist

Lillian Gish 1926 1984
Pencil on acid free matt board
39.6 x 37.6 cm
Inscribed: (l.r.) *Town Oct 29/84*
Not previously exhibited
The Artist

John Barrymore & Mary Astor in "Don Juan" 1926 1984
Pencil on acid free matt board
40.3 x 39.2 cm
Inscribed: (u.r.) *Nov 4/5 84*
Not previously exhibited
The Artist

Lon Chaney, The Phantom of the Opera, Universal 1925 1984
Pencil on acid free matt board
58.6 x 40.1 cm
Inscribed: (l.l.) *Town Nov. 8-84*
Not previously exhibited
The Artist

Joan Crawford & Constance Bennett at a Marion Davis Kiddie Party 1984
Pencil on acid free matt board
51.8 x 39.0 cm
Inscribed: (l.l.) *Town Nov. 20/84*
Not previously exhibited
The Artist

Rudolph Valentino, Monsieur Beaucaire 1984
Pencil on acid free matt board
56.2 x 38.4 cm
Inscribed: (u.r.) *Town Nov. 20/84*
Not previously exhibited
The Artist

Charlie Chaplin October 1925-To October 1927. The Circus 1984
Pencil on acid free matt board
58.0 x 40.0 cm
Inscribed: (l.r.) *Town Dec 5/84*
Not previously exhibited
The Artist

W.C. Fields & Mae West in "My Little Chickadee" 1985
Pencil on acid free matt board
46.1 x 54.7 cm
Inscribed: (l.l.) *Town Jan 12 85*
Not previously exhibited
The Artist

Sir Harry Lauder & Charlie Chaplin on the set of a British War Loan Short 1918 1985
Pencil on acid free matt board
41.0 x 34.1 cm
Inscribed: (l.r.) *Town Jan. 27-28.85*
Not previously exhibited
The Artist

Your Tooth in my neck - released as the "Fearless Vampire Killers" "Dance of the Vampires" Roman Polanski 1967 1985
Pencil on acid free matt board
47.7 x 62.7 cm
Inscribed: (l.l.) *Jan 29. Feb 4/85*
Not previously exhibited
The Artist

Bebe Davis & Gloria Swanson in "Why Change your Wife" 1920 1985
Pencil on acid free matt board
38.6 x 44.4 cm
Inscribed: (l.l.) *Town Feb 10/12 85*
Not previously exhibited
The Artist

Jacques Offenbach 1860 1985
Pencil on acid free matt board
50.5 x 34.2 cm
Inscribed: (l.r.) *Town Feb 26/85*
Not previously exhibited
The Artist

Stephane Mallarme 1842-98 1985
Pencil on acid free matt board
33.0 x 44.5 cm
Inscribed: (l.r.) *Town Feb 27-28/85*
Not previously exhibited
The Artist

Orson Welles 1979 1985
Pencil on acid free matt board
41.0 x 35.1 cm
Inscribed: (l.r.) *March 20/85*
Not previously exhibited
The Artist

"Follow the Boys" 1944, WC Fields & Bill Wolf 1985
Pencil on acid free matt board
25.1 x 33.9 cm
Inscribed: (l.r.) *Town March 28/85*
Not previously exhibited
The Artist

Betty Blythe in Queen of Sheba 1985
Pencil on acid free matt board
33.4 x 29.0 cm
Inscribed: (u.r.) *April 11-85*
Not previously exhibited
The Artist

Matzenhauer as Brünnhilde, Braun as Wotan at the Metropolitan c. 1890 1985
Pencil on acid free matt board
55.5 x 39.1 cm
Inscribed: (l.r.) *Town April-18-85*
Not previously exhibited
The Artist

Queen Victoria 1897 1985
Pencil on acid free matt board
37.8 x 40.0 cm
Inscribed: (l.r.) *Town May 1-2.85*
Not previously exhibited
The Artist

Piet Mondrian 1942 1985
Pencil on acid free matt board
43.2 x 34.4 cm
Inscribed: (l.l.) *May 8/85*
Not previously exhibited
The Artist

Herbert Kitchener and personal staff at Delhi-India-1902 1985
Pencil on acid free matt board
40.0 x 63.1 cm
Inscribed: (l.r.) *Town June 8/9/85*
Not previously exhibited
The Artist

Rasputin with Upper Class Ladies 1916 1985
Pencil on acid free matt board
50.9 x 32.8 cm
Inscribed: (l.l.) *Town June 11/85*
Not previously exhibited
The Artist

Abraham Lincoln, Nov. 8 1863, Washington D.C. 1985
Pencil on acid free matt board
36.7 x 30.6 cm
Inscribed: (l.r.) *Town July 18/24/85*
Not previously exhibited
The Artist

Oskar Kokoshka draws Ezra Pound 1985
Pencil on acid free matt board
34.6 x 37.4 cm
Inscribed: (l.r.) *Town Aug 21-85*
Not previously exhibited
The Artist

Degas in his studio wearing his painter's smock 1985
Pencil on acid free matt board
31.0 x 24.5 cm
Inscribed: (l.r.) *Town Aug 22/85*
Not previously exhibited
The Artist

Marlene Dietrich, The Devil is a Woman 1985
Pencil on acid free matt board
38.3 x 29.4 cm
Inscribed: (l.r.) *Town Sept 4/85*
Not previously exhibited
The Artist

LIST OF EXHIBITIONS

1946   *74th Annual Exhibition of the Ontario Society of Artists.* Art Gallery of Toronto. March 9 –April 13.

1948   *Mayfair Artists.* Toronto, The Fine Art Galleries, Eaton's College Street. September 29 – October 9.

1949   *77th Annual Exhibition of the Ontario Society of Artists.* Art Gallery of Toronto. March 5-27.

        Mayfair Artists. Toronto, The Fine Art Galleries, Eaton's College Street. June.

        Paintings and Sculptures for the Purchase Fund Sale 1949. Art Gallery of Toronto, Women's Committee. November 5-6.

1950   *Exhibition of Contemporary Canadian Arts.* Art Gallery of Toronto. March 3 – April 16.

        Exhibition of Unaffiliated Artists. Toronto, The Fine Art Galleries, Eaton's College Street. May 17.

        Third Annual Winter Exhibition. Art Gallery of Hamilton. December 2 – 31.

1951   *79th Annual Exhibition of the Ontario Society of Artists.* Art Gallery of Toronto. March 10 – April 15.

        2nd Annual Exhibition of Unaffiliated Artists. Toronto, The Fine Art Galleries, Eaton's College Street.

        Exhibition of Paintings and Sculpture. Toronto, Canadian National Exhibition. August 24 – September 8.

        72nd Annual Exhibition of the Royal Canadian Academy of Arts. Art Gallery of Toronto. November 23, 1951 – January 6, 1952.

        Graphic Art 1951. Canadian Society of Graphic Art. Circulated by the National Gallery of Canada.

        4th Annual Winter Exhibition. Art Gallery of Hamilton. December.

1952   *3rd Annual Exhibition of Unaffiliated Artists.* Art Gallery of Toronto. April 25 – June 1.

        Exhibition. Canadian Group of Painters. Art Gallery of Toronto. October – November. National tour 1953.

        Annual Sale of Canadian Art. Windsor, Willistead Art Gallery. November 14 – December 31.

        5th Annual Winter Exhibition. Art Gallery of Hamilton. December.

1953   *27th Annual Exhibition. Canadian Society for Painters in Watercolour.* Art Gallery of Toronto. January 9 – February 22.

        Annual Exhibition of Canadian Painting. Ottawa, National Gallery of Canada. March.

        Opening Exhibition. Ottawa, Robertson Galleries. March 24 – April 28.

        Canadian Society of Graphic Art. Ottawa, National Gallery of Canada. May.

        4th Annual Exhibition and Sale of Canadian Art. Windsor, Willistead Art Gallery. November 20 – December 30.

        Exhibition of Paintings and Sculpture. Toronto, Canadian National Exhibition. August 28 – September 12.

1954   *Young Contemporaries.* London, Ontario, Elsie Perrin Williams Memorial Art Gallery. January.

        Painters 11. Toronto, Roberts Gallery. February 13-27; Ottawa, Robertson Galleries. March – April.

        82nd Annual Exhibition of the Ontario Society of Artists. Art Gallery of Toronto. February 26 – March 28.

Drawings and Graphics 1947 - 1954. Kazuo Nakamura, Harold Town, Oscar Cahén. Toronto, Eglinton Gallery. May.

Exhibition of Paintings and Sculpture. Toronto, Canadian National Exhibition. August 27 - September 11.

8th Annual Sale of Canadian Art. Art Gallery of Toronto, Women's Committee. October 22 - November 2.

Canadian Group of Painters. Exhibition 1954 - 55. Art Gallery of Toronto. November - December. National tour 1955.

6th Annual Winter Exhibition. Art Gallery of Hamilton. December.

1955   *83rd Annual Exhibition of the Ontario Society of Artists.* Art Gallery of Toronto. January 7 - February 9.

7th Annual Winter Exhibition. Art Gallery of Hamilton. December.

Painters Eleven. Toronto, Roberts Gallery. February 11 - 26; Oshawa, YWCA (Adelaide House). March - April.

Exhibition '55. Canadian Society of Graphic Art. Ottawa, National Gallery of Canada. May.

29th Annual Exhibition. Canadian Society for Painters in Watercolour. Art Gallery of Toronto. May.

First Biennial Exhibition of Canadian Painting. Ottawa, National Gallery of Canada. May.

Exhibition of Paintings and Sculpture. Toronto, Canadian National Exhibition. August 26 - September 10.

The Winnipeg Show. The Winnipeg Art Gallery. November 2 - 15.

Exhibition of Canadian Artists. Toronto, Woodsworth House. December.

Painters Eleven Exhibition 1956. St. Catharines, Public Library Art Gallery. December 1955 - January 1956. Ontario tour.

1956   *84th Annual Exhibition of the Ontario Society of Artists.* Art Gallery of Toronto. February 17 - March 18.

Small Pictures by Painters Eleven. Toronto, Roberts Gallery. February 28 - March 7.

20th Annual Exhibition of American Abstract Artists with Painters Eleven of Canada. New York, Riverside Museum. April 8 - May 20.

Four Canadians. Art Gallery of Toronto. May 4 - June 3.

Painters Eleven Small Originals. Oshawa, Pauline's Giftland. May.

Exhibition of Paintings and Sculpture. Toronto, Canadian National Exhibition. August 24 - September 8.

XXVIII Biennale di Venezia. Venice, Italy. June 16 - October 21.

Painters Eleven. Toronto, Arts and Letters Club. September 15 - October 30.

10th Annual Sale of Contemporary Canadian Art. Art Gallery of Toronto, Women's Committee. October 26 - November 5.

The 2nd Winnipeg Show. The Winnipeg Art Gallery. November 4-25.

Exhibition of Canadian Art. Toronto, Grand & Toy; Sponsored by Grand and Toy and *The Globe and Mail.* November 27 - December 22.

Canadian Abstract Paintings. Organized by the National Gallery of Canada for circulation in the United States by the Smithsonian Institution.

1957   *85th Annual Exhibition of the Ontario Society of Artists.* Art Gallery of Toronto. March 9 - April 7.

IIe exposition internationale de gravure. Ljubljana, Yugoslavia, Moderna Galerija. July 18 - September 15.

Triennial de Milano. Milan, Italy.

IV Bienal. São Paulo, Brazil, Museu de Arte Moderna. September – December.

2nd Sale of Fine Arts. Art Gallery of Hamilton, Women's Committee. September 20-29.

Painters Eleven 1957 Exhibition. Toronto, The Park Gallery. October 31 – November 16.

11th Annual Sale of Canadian Art. Art Gallery of Toronto, Women's Committee. October 24 – November 11.

3rd Winnipeg Show. The Winnipeg Art Gallery. November.

Eighth Annual Exhibition and Sale of Canadian Art. Windsor, Willistead Art Gallery. November 27 – December 4.

7 Canadians: Paintings and Sculptures. Toronto, Gallery of Contemporary Art. December 4 – 31.

1958   *9th Annual Winter Exhibition.* Art Gallery of Hamilton. February.

Salon of Canadian Artists. Toronto, Jordan Gallery. March 15-29.

V Mostra Internazionale di Bianco e Nero. Lugano, Switzerland. April 3 – June 15.

Painters Eleven 1958. Montreal, École des beaux-arts. May 3-23. Smaller version circulated nationally by the National Gallery of Canada as *1958 - 59 Painters Eleven.*

1958 Biennial: Paintings, Prints, Sculpture. Minneapolis, Minnesota, Walker Art Center. May 4 – June 15.

Art contemporain au Canada. Brussels, Belgium, Palais des beaux-arts. May 13 – June 1.

Painters Eleven. Hamilton, The Alan Gallery. May 30 – June 19.

1st International Triennial of Original Coloured Graphics. Grenchen, Switzerland, Parktheater. June 14 – July 12.

Canada at Brussels. Brussels, Belgium, World Fair.

Exhibition of Paintings and Sculpture. Toronto, Canadian National Exhibition. August 20 – September 6.

A Canadian Portfolio. Texas, Dallas Museum of Contemporary Arts. September 4 –November 2.

Canadian Group of Painters Exhibition 1958. Vancouver Art Gallery. September 9 –October 5.

Points of View. London Public Library and Art Museum. October 17 – November 26, Ontario tour.

Annual Exhibition. Vancouver Art Gallery, Women's Auxiliary. October 18-22.

International Festival of Art. New York, Festival Galleries. October 24 – November 23.

Painters Eleven with Ten Distinguished Artists from Quebec. Toronto, The Park Gallery. October 31 – November 15.

Moderne canadese schilderkunst. Utrecht, the Netherlands, Centraal Museum. November 7 – December 7; the Netherlands, Groningen Museum. December 12, 1958 – January 12, 1959.

4th Winnipeg Show. The Winnipeg Art Gallery.

1959   *10th Annual Winter Exhibition.* Art Gallery of Hamilton. February.

Art contemporain au Canada. Geneva, Switzerland, Musée Rath. February 7 – March 1; Cologne, West Germany, Wallraf-Richartz Museum (as *Zeitgenössische Kunst in Kanada*). March 14 – April 12.

87th Annual Exhibition of the Ontario Society of Artists. Art Gallery of Toronto. March 21 – April 19.

20th Biennial International Watercolor Exhibition. New York, The Brooklyn Museum. April 7 – May 31.

IIIe exposition internationale de gravure. Ljubljana, Yugoslavia, Moderna Galerija. June 7 – September 15.

Images du Canada: A Small Exhibition of Canadian Graphic Art. Aspen, Colorado. International Design Conference. June.

Ten Canadians. Stratford, The Stratford Festival Art Exhibition.

Summer Exhibition. Toronto, Edwards Gardens.

Private Collectors Choice in Canadian Art. Toronto, Canadian National Exhibition. August 26 – September 12.

3rd Sale of Fine Arts. Art Gallery of Hamilton, Women's Committee. September 18-27.

Canadian Watercolours and Graphics Today. American Federation of the Arts, Extension Services. October 1959 – October 1960.

80th Annual Exhibition of the Royal Canadian Academy. Quebec Musée de la Province. November 6-30, 1959; Winnipeg, Civic Auditorium. January 3-27, 1960.

The Third Biennial of Canadian Art. Ottawa, National Gallery of Canada. June 11 – July 5.

Savremena kanadska grafika. Belgrade and Ljubljana, Yugoslavia.

Canadian Group of Painters. Exhibition 1959. Art Gallery of Toronto. November – December 1959; Fredericton, Beaverbrook Art Gallery. February 1960.

1960   *11th Annual Winter Exhibition.* Art Gallery of Hamilton. February.

88th Annual Exhibition of the Ontario Society of Artists. Art Gallery of Toronto. March 26 – April 24.

The 1960 International Biennial of Prints. Ohio, Cincinnati Art Museum. April 1 – May 22.

3rd Annual Exhibition and Sale of Works by Leading Canadian Artists from Coast to Coast. Ottawa Section of the National Council of Jewish Women of Canada. April 6-7.

Painters Eleven. Montreal, The Stable Gallery, The Montreal Museum of Fine Arts. April 8-30.

77th Annual Spring Exhibition. The Montreal Museum of Fine Arts. April 8 – May 8.

Five Painters from Canada. New York, Guggenheim International Exhibition.

14th Annual Exhibition and Sale of Contemporary Canadian Paintings, Sculptures and Graphics. Art Gallery of Toronto, Women's Committee. November 3-20.

Arte canadiense. Organized by the National Gallery of Canada for Museo de Arte Moderno, Mexico City. November.

Painters Eleven Exhibition. Kitchener – Waterloo Art Gallery. December 2, 1960 –January 15.

1961   *4th Annual Exhibition and Sale of Works by Leading Canadian Artists from Coast to Coast.* Ottawa Section of the National Council of Jewish Women of Canada. April 19-20.

The Fourth Biennial of Canadian Art. Ottawa, National Gallery of Canada. May 19 – September 4.

8 Canadian Artists. Montreal, Galerie Dresdnere. May 31 – June 10.

IVe exposition internationale de gravure. Ljubljana, Yugoslavia, Moderna Galerija. June 11 – September 15.

The Creative Spirit of Canada. Pennsylvania, Pittsburgh International Arts Festival. June.

VI Bienal. São Paulo, Brazil, Museu de Arte Moderna. September – December.

4th Biennial Sale of Fine Arts. Art Gallery of Hamilton, Women's Committee. September 23 – October 1.

15th Annual Exhibition and Sale of Contemporary Canadian Paintings, Sculpture and Graphics. Art Gallery of Toronto, Women's Committee. November 1-19.

Six Graphic Artists. Hart House, University of Toronto. November 21 – December 3.

Toronto '61. Toronto Board of Education. National tour 1961-62.

1962   *79th Annual Spring Exhibition.* The Montreal Museum of Fine Arts. April 7 – May 6.

The Ernie Taylor Benefit Exhibition. Art Gallery of Toronto. April 18 – May 6.

Jock Macdonald, Harold Town, Dennis Burton. Toronto, O'Keefe Centre. May.

Art of the Americas. New York, The Trabia-Morris Gallery. October 16 – November 10.

16th Annual Exhibition and Sale of Contemporary Canadian Paintings, Sculptures and Graphics. Art Gallery of Toronto, Women's Committee. October 18 – November 4.

19 Canadian Painters 1962. Louisville, Kentucky, The J.B. Speed Art Museum. October 23 – November 25.

Commonwealth Art Today. London, England, Commonwealth Institute. November 7, 1962 – January 13, 1963.

Canadian Prints. New York, Pratt Graphic Art Centre.

Nowoczesne malarstwo kanadijskie. Warsaw, Poland, Museum Narodowe w warszawie.

International Exhibition. Tunis, Tunisian Artists Association.

3rd International Biennial Exhibition of Prints. Tokyo, Japan.

New Acquisitions. New York, The Museum of Modern Art. December.

1963   *83rd Annual Exhibition of the Royal Canadian Academy.* Art Gallery of Toronto. January 11 – February 10.

Contemporary Canadian Painting and Sculpture. New York, Rochester Memorial Art Gallery. January 25 – February 24.

Toronto Painters and Sculptors Exhibition. Toronto, Glenhyrst Gardens. February 15 – March 10.

80th Annual Spring Exhibition. The Montreal Museum of Fine Arts. April.

Sculpture. Toronto, Jerrold Morris International Gallery.

Mixed Media and Pop Art. Buffalo, New York, Albright-Knox Art Gallery. November 19 –December 15.

Arte de America y Espana. Madrid, Spain, Instituto de Cultura Hispanica. May – June. International tour.

Cézanne and Structure in Modern Painting. New York, Solomon R. Guggenheim Museum. June – August.

Ve exposition internationale de gravure. Ljubljana, Yugoslavia, Moderna Galerija. June 9 – September 15; as *Graphik 63.* Vienna, Austria, Graphische Sammlung, Albertina. October 21 – December 22.

Dunn International. Fredericton, Beaverbrook Art Gallery. September 7 – October 6; London, England, The Tate Gallery. November 15 – December 22.

The Art of Things. Toronto, Jerrold Morris International Gallery. October.

Quebec – Ontario, 1963, 17th Annual Exhibition and Sale of Contemporary Canadian Art. Art Gallery of Toronto, Women's Committee. October 25 – November 11.

la Bienal Americana de Grabado. Santiago, Chile, Museo de Arte Contemporaneo, Universidad de Chile. November 20 – December 21.

Fifteen Canadian Artists. New York, The Museum of Modern Art, International Council; circulated in the United States, 1963-1964.

5th Biennial of Canadian Art. Ottawa, National Gallery of Canada. September 20 – October 27.

12th Exhibition of Contemporary American Painting and Sculpture. Toronto. The Jerrold Morris International Gallery.

2 Sculptors, 4 Painters. New York, Galeria Bonino. December 18, 1963 – January 11, 1964.

1964   *84th Annual Exhibition of the Royal Canadian Academy.* Ottawa, National Gallery of Canada. January 16 – February 9.

Canadian Painting 1939-1963. Organized by the National Gallery of Canada for London, England, The Tate Gallery. February – March.

Canadian Sculpture Today. Toronto, The Dorothy Cameron Gallery. Part 1, March 20 – April 5; Part 2, April 10-26.

Some Toronto Painters 1950 - 64. Art Gallery of Toronto. April 3 – May 3.

Documenta III. Internationale Ausstellung. Kassel, West Germany, Museum Fredericianum. June 27 - October 5.

World Show. New York, Washington Square Gallery. July.

The Corporation Collects. Toronto, Arthur White Gallery. September 3-24.

New Originals: Contemporary Canadian Drawings and Prints. Toronto, The Art Institute of Ontario. September.

Exhibition of Contemporary Painting and Sculpture: Pittsburgh International 1964. Pittsburgh, Pennsylvania, Carnegie Institute, Museum of Art. October 30, 1964 - January 10, 1965.

Canadian Art Today III. Kitchener-Waterloo, University of Waterloo, Gallery of Theatre Arts.

Canadian Drawings and Prints. London, Ontario, London Public Art Museum. December.

1965   *International '65. A Selection from the 1964 Pittsburg International. Part One.* Detroit, Michigan, J.L. Hudson Gallery. February 10 – March 6.

Art and Engineering. Art Gallery of Toronto. February 13 – March 13.

Spring Arts Festival. Toronto, Holy Blossom Temple. April.

Canadian Printmaking Today. Toronto, Dorothy Cameron Gallery. April 2-26.

Eros '65. Toronto, The Dorothy Cameron Gallery. June.

(Sculpture). Stratford, Shakespeare Festival Theatre.

Sixth Biennial Exhibition of Canadian Painting. Ottawa, National Gallery of Canada. June 4 – August 22.

Canadian Drawings and Prints. Penarth, Wales, Turner House, Cardiff Commonwealth Arts Festival. September 18 – October 10.

Art Loan Society. Port Credit. October 22-23.

Focus on Drawings. Art Gallery of Toronto, Women's Committee. October 15 – November 7.

25 Ontario Painters of the 20th Century. St. Catharines, Rodman Hall Arts Centre. October 24 – November 21.

Print Biennale. Prague, Czechoslovakia.

1+1 = 3 Retinal. Austin, Texas.

Contemporary American Painting and Sculpture. Chicago, University of Illinois.

Canadian Graphic Art. London, England, Victoria and Albert Museum for tour in UK.

Segunda Bienal Americana de Grabado. Santiago, Chile, Museo de Arte Contemporaneo, Universidad de Chile.

VIe exposition internationale de gravure. Ljubljana, Yugoslavia, Moderna Galerija.

The Brock Hall Collection. Vancouver, University of British Columbia and Vancouver Art Gallery.

Mir' humanost in prijateljstvo med narodi. Slovenijagradec, Yugoslavia, Galerija Moderne umetnosti. December.

1966   *Drawings by Nine Canadians.* Kingston, Agnes Etherington Art Centre, Queen's University. January 16 – February 13.

Contemporary Woman. University of Toronto, University College. January.

17th Annual Winter Exhibition. Art Gallery of Hamilton. February.

Satirical Art. Toronto, York University. March.

Canadian Religious Art Today. Willowdale, Regis College. April 12 – May 2.

Visua '66. Canadian Critics' Choice. Pointe-Claire, Quebec. Fairview Shopping Centre. May 5-31.

A Bit of the Cream of Canadian Art. Vancouver, The Studio Art Gallery International. May 10 – 31.

Modern Painting. University of Toronto, Scarborough College.

Royal Canadian Academy: The Academy in Retrospect 1966. Charlottetown, Confederation Centre Art Gallery and Museum. July – September.

Recent Acquisitions, Painting and Sculpture. New York, Museum of Modern Art.

Canadian Watercolours, Drawings and Prints. Ottawa, National Gallery of Canada.

Collector Finds. Davenport, Iowa, Davenport Municipal Art Gallery.

le Biennale Internationale de la Gravure. Cracow, Poland.

1967   *Centennial Exhibition of Quebec and Ontario Contemporary Painters 1967.* Kitchener – Waterloo Art Gallery. February 4-26. National tour.

The Men Choose: an Exhibition and Sale. Toronto, Art Gallery of Ontario, Women's Committee. February 10 – March 5.

Alumni Hall Opening. London, University of Western Ontario. March.

Prize Award Winners 1908-1965. The Montreal Museum of Fine Arts. March 30 – April 30.

Contemporary Canadian Prints and Drawings in Australia 1967-68. Organized by the National Gallery of Canada for Australian tour. March 1967 – November 1968.

Twenty Canadians. Vancouver, Douglas Gallery. April.

Canada 67 Exhibition. New York, Museum of Modern Art. May 2 – June 4.

Three Hundred Years of Canadian Art. Ottawa, National Gallery of Canada. May 12 – September 17.

Eleven Canadian Printmakers. Hanover, New Hampshire, Hopkins Center Art Galleries, Dartmouth College. April 5-23; Lincoln, Massachusetts, DeCordova Museum. May 4 – June 18.

Canadian Sculpture 1967. Ottawa, Blue Barn Gallery. April 12 – May 6.

Painting in Canada. Montreal, Expo '67, The Canadian Government Pavilion. April 28 –October 27.

Canadian Prints and Drawings. Montreal, Expo 67, Canadian Government Pavilion. April 28 – October 27.

Expo 67. Montreal. Ontario Pavilion. April 28 – October 27.

4th National Burnaby Print Show. Burnaby Art Society. June 10 – July 3.

Canadian Art of Our Time. The Winnipeg Art Gallery. June 22 – August 31.

One Hundred Years of Theatre in Canada. Stratford.

Director's Choice. Charlottetown, Confederation Centre. Charlottetown Summer Festival. July 4 – September 3.

Vancouver Print International. Vancouver Art Gallery. October 5-29.

1968   *Douglas Duncan's Private Collection.* Art Gallery of Hamilton. January 6-22.

20 Painters. Montreal, Galerie du Siècle. January.

Survey 68/Sondage 68. Montreal Museum of Fine Arts. March 8 – April 7.

Concours d'Elegance: Black and White. Toronto, Jerrold Morris Gallery. May 4-22.

The Alexandra Luke Collection. Oshawa, The Robert McLaughlin Gallery. May 7-26.

Exposition de peintures canadiennes contemporains. Montreal, Centre d'art du Mont-Royal. June 20 – September 2.

Seventh Biennial of Canadian Painting. Ottawa, National Gallery of Canada. July 4 – September 1.

C.S. Band Collection of Drawings. Toronto, Art Gallery of Ontario. July 20 – September 8.

Canada 101. The Second Edinburgh Hundred. Edinburgh, Scotland, The Edinburgh School of Art. August 18 – September 7.

Hart House Collects: Recent Acquisitions. Ottawa, National Gallery of Canada. National tour 1968-69.

1969   *Canadian Printmakers.* University of Guelph. May 2-26.

The Road to Expansion. The Montreal Museum of Fine Arts. October 22 – November 16.

The Collection of the Canada Council. Ottawa, National Gallery of Canada. Travelling Exhibition 1969-71.

Festival 68 Exhibitions. Edinburgh, Scotland, The Richard Delmarco Gallery. 1969.

Contemporary Canadians. Winnipeg, Winnipeg Art Gallery. July – August 1969.

Canadian Art for Collectors. Windsor, Art Gallery of Windsor. November 16 – 30, 1969.

British International Print Biennial. England, Bradford City Art Gallery. November 28, 1968 – January 19, 1969.

Primera Bienal Interamericana de Pinture y Grabado. Mexico, Instituto Nacional de Bellas Artes. June 6 – August 20.

Art for Architecture. Toronto, Art Gallery of Ontario, Extension Exhibition.

1970   Canadian Pavilion, Expo 70. Osaka, Japan. March 15 – September 13.

Coltejer Second Biennial of Art. Medellin, Colombia. May 1 – June 15.

Works (Mostly) on Paper – Drawing Reconsidered. Boston, Massachusetts, Institute of Contemporary Art. October 21 – November 14.

Canadian Art for Collectors. Art Gallery of Windsor. November 15-22.

Exhibition of Paintings: Royal Canadian Academy. Atlantic Provinces Art Circuit, 1970-71.

1971   *Painters Eleven: 1953-1960.* Oshawa, The Robert McLaughlin Gallery. February 24 – March 14.

Canadian Art for Collectors. Art Gallery of Windsor. November 14-21.

6th Burnaby Print Show. Burnaby Art Gallery. November 4 – December 5.

1972   *Art of the XXth Century.* The Montreal Museum of Fine Arts. January 14 – February 20.

International Graphic Exhibition. Vancouver, Galerie Allen in collaboration with the David Ash Gallery, Seattle, Washington. April 12 – May 2.

(Graphics Exhibition). Venice, Italy, Museo d'arte moderna. June.

Painters Eleven 1953-1959. Parts A and B. Oshawa, The Robert McLaughlin Gallery. Travelling exhibition, 1972-73.

Toronto Painting: 1953-1965. Ottawa, National Gallery of Canada. September 15 – October 15; Toronto, Art Gallery of Ontario. November 10 – December 10.

Ontario Society of Artists. 100 Years 1872-1972. Toronto, Art Gallery of Ontario. September 16 - October 29. Ontario tour.

1st International Print Exhibition. Rizal, Philippines. Galerie Bleue. December 20, 1972 - January 8, 1973.

1973   *Art for All.* Art Gallery of Windsor. October 21 - November 2.

1974   *A Tribute to Hieronymous Bosch.* University of Waterloo Art Gallery. January 13 - February 3.

Art for All. Art Gallery of Windsor. November 8 - December 1.

1975   *Painters Eleven.* Owen Sound, The Tom Thomson Memorial Gallery and Museum of Fine Art. November 7-30; Sudbury Arts Festival 'Spectrum 75'. October 10-19.

Art for All. Art Gallery of Windsor. November 6-27.

The Ontario Community Collects: A Survey of Canadian Painting from 1766 to the Present. Toronto, Art Gallery of Ontario. December 12, 1975 - February 1, 1976.

1976   *Arnold Bode zum 75 Geburtstag.* Kassel, West Germany, Kasseler Kunstverein.

Selections from the Moore Collection. London Regional Art Gallery. March.

Contemporary Canadian Poster Art. Ottawa, SAW Gallery. March 22 - April 3.

Through Canadian Eyes: Trends and Influences in Canadian Art 1815-1965. Calgary, Glenbow-Alberta Institute.

Painters Eleven. Kitchener-Waterloo Art Gallery. November 4-28.

100 Years: Evolution of the Ontario College of Art. Toronto, The Art Gallery of Ontario. November 5, 1976 - January 2, 1977. Circulated.

Art for All. Art Gallery of Windsor. November 7-26.

Horse Show. Toronto, Gadatsy Gallery. November 30 - December 17.

1977   *Canadian Tapestries 1977.* Toronto, Art Gallery of Ontario. June 4 - July 24.

1978   *Painters Eleven.* Stratford, The Gallery/Stratford. March 29 - April 9.

Works by Painters Eleven: 1953-60 from The Robert McLaughlin Gallery. Toronto, York University, Glendon Gallery. July 7 - August 11.

Painters Eleven. 25 Years. Oshawa, The Robert McLaughlin Gallery. September 6 - October 14.

Art for All. Art Gallery of Windsor. November 5-24.

Selected Drawings: The Figure. Guelph, McLaughlin Library, University of Guelph. October 12 - November 22.

1979   *Pasted Paper: A Look at Canadian Collage 1955-1965.* Kingston, Agnes Etherington Art Centre, Queen's University. May 19 - June 30.

20th-Century Canadian Drawings. Stratford: The Gallery/Stratford. June 14 - September 3.

Art for All. Art Gallery of Windsor. November 4-25.

Painters Eleven in Retrospect. Oshawa: The Robert McLaughlin Gallery. October 30 - December 2. National tour through 1981.

1980   *An Exhibition of Works Donated by the Alumni of Sir George Williams University and Loyola College to The Concordia University Collection of Art.* Montreal, Concordia University, Sir George Williams Art Galleries. April 10-29.

Art for All. Art Gallery of Windsor. November 2-21.

Art for Rent: Works for Public Places from the Canada Council Art Bank. Toronto, Harbourfront Art Gallery. February 22 - March 23.

Canadian Treasures: 25 Artists, Paintings, Years. Kitchener-Waterloo Art Gallery. October 8, 1980 – January 11, 1981.

1982   *The Essential Line: Art and Purpose in Drawing.* Charlottetown, Confederation Centre Art Gallery and Museum. April 7 – May 23.

Art for Architecture: Selections from the Government of Ontario Art Collection 1966-1981. Toronto, Macdonald Gallery. May 27 – July 4.

Art for All. Art Gallery of Windsor. November 7-26.

1983   *Toronto Painting of the 1960s.* Toronto, Art Gallery of Ontario Extension Services. Ontario tour and Mexico City, Museo de Arte Carillo Gil. 1983-1984.

Art for All. Art Gallery of Windsor. November 6-27.

1985   *The Zacks Gift: Then & Now.* Kingston, Agnes Etherington Art Centre, Queen's University. October 26 – December 24.

SOLO AND TWO-PERSON EXHIBITIONS

1954   *Prints.* Toronto, Picture Loan Society.

1955   *One Man Show: Recent Colour Print Collages.* Toronto, Helene Arthur Upstairs Gallery. October 7-31.

Harold Town-Autographic Prints. Toronto, Little Jack's, Lawrence Plaza. December.

1956   *Single Autographic Prints. Harold Town.* Toronto, Picture Loan Society. November 24 – December 7.

1957   *Harold Town.* Toronto, Gallery of Contemporary Art. January 22 – February 6.

Autographic Prints by Harold Town. Montreal, Galerie L'Actuelle. March 12-26.

Harold Town Exhibition. Ottawa, George Loranger Gallery. May.

1958   *Two Canadian Painters: Paul-Emile Borduas and Harold Town.* London, England, Arthur Tooth and Sons Ltd. October 7-25.

1959   *Town Collages.* Toronto, Jordan Gallery. January 22 – February 14.

An Exhibition of Drawings by Harold Town. Toronto, Laing Galleries. September 19 – October 2.

1960   *Harold Town: Collages, Paintings, Prints, Drawings.* Regina, Norman Mackenzie Art Gallery, Regina College. January 12 – February 3.

Salon d'automne: Nakamura and Harold Town. The Montreal Museum of Fine Arts, October – November.

1961   *Harold Town: Paintings, Collages, Prints.* Toronto, Laing Galleries. February 25 – March 8.

Harold Town. Montreal, Galerie Dresdnere. December 9-23.

1962   *Harold Town.* Kitchener-Waterloo Art Gallery. January 5-28.

Harold Town: New Paintings, Collages, Drawings. Toronto, Jerrold Morris International Gallery. April 13 – May 5.

Harold Town Autographic Prints. Toronto, Towne Cinema. August.

Town. New York, Andrew-Morris Gallery. November 20, 1962 – January 3, 1963.

1963   *Town: An Exhibition of Recent Paintings of the Theme of "The Tyranny of the Corner."* Madison, Fairleigh Dickinson University. February 2-18; New Jersey Museum of Arts. March.

1964   *Harold Town Retrospective: 80 Drawings 1952-64.* Toronto, Jerrold Morris International Gallery. March 5-25.

XXXII Biennale de Venezia: Harold Town and Elza Mayhew. Venice, Italy. June 20 – October 18.

Harold Town Retrospective: Figurative Drawings 1949-63. Montreal, Gallery Dresdnere. September 22 – October 6.

Thirteen Paintings by Harold Town. Vancouver Art Gallery. October 9 – November 1.

Harold Town Paintings. New York, Galeria Bonino. October 13 – November 7.

1965   *Harold Town.* Scarborough Public Library, Bendale Branch. April 22 – May 15.

Harold Town Retrospective 1955-65. Vancouver, The Studio Art Gallery International. December 4-31.

1966   *Harold Town.* Chicago, Sears Vincent Price Gallery. January 25 – February 25.

Harold Town: Paintings 1964. Toronto, Mazelow Gallery. January 29 – February 19.

Harold Town: Paintings, 1965. Toronto, Jerrold Morris International Gallery. January 29 – February 19.

Harold Town. Ottawa, The Blue Barn Gallery. April 6-30.

Harold Town: Drawings and Prints. Guelph, Macdonald Institute, University of Guelph. April 11-30.

Single Autographic Prints and Drawings in Brush, Pen and Ink. Waterloo, University of Waterloo, The Kitchener-Waterloo Art Gallery and the Gallery of the Theatre of the Arts. May.

Harold Town. Montreal, Waddington Galleries. June 1-18.

1967   *Harold Town Paintings.* Scarborough College, University of Toronto. January 9-31.

Exhibition of Autographic Prints. Toronto, Hart House, University of Toronto. January 9-22.

Harold Town. Chicago, Sears Vincent Price Gallery. January 25 – February 25.

A Retrospective of Oils 1960-1965. Vancouver, The Douglas Gallery. January 25 – February 9.

Harold Town: Prints, drawings and watercolours. Winnipeg, Yellow Door Gallery. February.

Harold Town. Calgary, Kensington Gallery. 1967.

Jean McEwen and Harold Town. Ottawa, National Gallery of Canada, Extension Services. Circulated in Canada and US 1966-67.

Harold Town: 1954/1959. Prints and Collages. Toronto, Mazelow Gallery and Jerrold Morris Gallery. November 25 – December 31.

1968   *Smokes and Other Drawings.* Toronto, Winters College, York University. October.

Harold Town. Chicago, Sears Vincent Price Gallery. November 7 – December 7.

1969   *Harold Town: Enigmas.* Toronto, Hart House, University of Toronto. January.

New Town Enigmas. Toronto, Mazelow Gallery. April 12 – May 10.

New Town Enigmas and Other Recent Drawings. Windsor, Willistead Art Gallery. May 22 – June 15.

Harold Town Enigmas. Chicago, Sears Vincent Price Gallery.

Retrospective Exhibition to Mark the Publication of "Drawings by Harold Town." Toronto, Mazelow Gallery. November 11-29.

Harold Town, Montreal, Waddington Gallery. November 11-29.

Harold Town. Bedford, Canadian Galleries, Ten Mile House. November.

Pop Musicians. Toronto, Jerrold Morris Gallery.

1970   *Harold Town Enigmas.* Toronto, Hart House, University of Toronto. January 4-23.

   Harold Town Single Autographic Prints. Toronto, Vanier Art Gallery, York University.

   Retrospective Drawing Exhibition. Art Gallery of Windsor. February 1-28.

   Harold Town: Exhibition of Drawings. Toronto, Imperial Cinema. April 20.

   Harold Town: Drawings 1947-70. Montreal, Waddington Galleries. May 19 – June 6.

   Harold Town: Paintings. Ontario Place. Toronto, Mazelow Gallery. December 2-30.

1971   *Harold Town: Popsters and Celebrities.* Atlantic Provinces Arts Circuit. June 1971 – May 1972.

   French Postcard Set - Girl on a Bicycle. Winnipeg, Fleet Galleries. September 22 – October 20.

   Silent Stars, Sound Stars, Film Stars. Stratford, Ontario, Rothman's Art Gallery. May 1-25.

   Silent Stars, Sound Stars, Film Stars. Chicago, Sears Vincent Price Gallery. October 15 – November 6; Toronto, Mazelow Gallery. November 16 – December 11; Detroit, Michigan, London Fine Arts. January 1972.

   Harold Town: Prints. Sarnia Public Library and Art Gallery. December.

1972   *Harold Town: Recent Paintings.* Montreal, Waddington Galleries. March 15 – April 1.

   Harold Town Drawings: French Postcards. Toronto, Mazelow Gallery. April 29 – May 27.

   Harold Town – A Selection. Cobourg, Art Gallery of Northumberland. June 9-24.

   William Nathanial Bird Everton and Drawings by Harold Barling Town. Toronto, Mazelow Gallery. December 22, 1972 – January 8, 1973.

1973   *Harold Town: Recent Drawings and Prints.* London, Ontario, Thielsen Art Gallery. January 27 – February 9.

   Harold Town: French Postcard Series. Vancouver, Bau-Xi Gallery. February 12 – March 2.

   Harold Town: The First Exhibition of New Work, 1969-1973. Oshawa, The Robert McLaughlin Gallery. May 15 – June 24. Ontario tour.

   Harold Town: Enigmas. Toronto, Gadatsy Gallery. September 15 – October 4.

   Harold Town. Hamilton, Damkjar-Burton Galleries. September 25 – October 6.

   French Postcard Series. Ottawa, Wallack Galleries. November – December.

   Snaps/73: New Paintings by Harold Town. Toronto, Mazelow Gallery. December 4, 1973 – January 3, 1974.

1974   *Harold Town.* Oakville, Gairloch Gardens. January 26 – February 24.

   Harold Town Lithographs and Serigraphs. Toronto, Mazelow Gallery. March 30 – April 18.

   Harold Town: Recent Paintings. Montreal, Waddington Galleries. March 2-30.

   Vale Variations 72/73/74. Toronto, Mazelow Gallery. May 21 – June 15.

   Harold Town "Dining Room Drawings." Hamilton, Damkjar-Burton Gallery. November 1-16.

   Harold Town Recent "Dining Room Drawings." Toronto, Gadatsy Gallery. November 23 – December 5.

1975   *Indications. Paintings, Collages, Drawings, Prints, Sculpture. Harold Town 1944-1975.* Art Gallery of Windsor. September 27 – October 22; Sarnia Public Library and Art Gallery. October 31 – November 25. A reduced version was shown in the Macdonald Block, Queen's Park, Toronto, December 16, 1975 – January 15, 1976, as *Harold Town: 1944-1975 (an exhibition of the art of Harold Town).*

   Harold Town: New Paintings 1973-75. Toronto, Mazelow Gallery. October 1-18.

   Recent Vale Variations. Toronto, Gadatsy Gallery. November 11-29.

1976   *Harold Town Drawings and Sybil Calverley Watercolours.* Georgetown, Gallery House Sol. March 27 – April 15.

1977   *Harold Town. Vale Variations.* Montreal, Waddington Galleries. November 30 - December 23.

1978   *Harold Town. The Toy Horse. Works on Paper.* Montreal, Waddington Galleries. April 20 –May 10.

        The Toy Horse. Works on Paper. Ottawa, Robertson Galleries. September 28 - October 19.

1979   *Harold Town: Paintings 1961.* Montreal, Waddington Galleries.

        Vale Variations. Ottawa, Robertson Galleries. November 24 - December 7.

1980   *Harold Town: "The God Drawings."* Toronto, Waddington Galleries. March 8 - April 16; Montreal, Waddington Galleries.

        Poets and Other People: Drawings by Harold Town. Art Gallery of Windsor. September 28 - October 26.

1981   *Harold Town: Recent Paintings.* Toronto, Waddington Galleries. May 14 - June 4.

        Portrait Drawings by Harold Town. Hamilton, Moore Gallery. October 29 - November 21.

1982   *Portrait Drawings by Harold Town.* Ottawa, Robertson Galleries. March 18 - April 2.

1984   *Toy Horse Drawings by Harold Town.* Moore Gallery, Hamilton, exhibition held at Laing Galleries, Toronto. February 22 - March 4.

1985   *Harold Town: Bug Drawings.* Toronto, Bau-Xi Gallery. April 20 - May 9.

        Harold Town: The Toy Horse. Vancouver, Bau-Xi Gallery. October 28 - November 9.

PHOTO CREDITS

Howard T. Agriesti, Sarasota, Florida: p. 169; Art Gallery of Hamilton: pp. 131, 174; Art Gallery of Ontario: p. 34; Art Gallery of Ontario, Brenda Dereniuk: pp. 6, 7, 58, 68, 91, 92, 136, 141, 145, 149, 151, 154, 159, 163, 165, 166, 172, 179, 191, 192, 201, 204, 209, 210; Art Gallery of Ontario, Bill Wilson: pp. 9, 207, 208; Jim Chambers: pp. 27, 28, 35, 39, 42, 43, 71, 78, 83, 97, 114, 119, 120, 127, 154, 155, 181; Don Hall (A-V Services), University of Regina: p. 101; Grant Hill Photography, Inc., Sarnia: p. 30; Robert Keziere, Vancouver: pp. 15, 108, 125, 161, 164; William Kuryluk, London, Ontario: p. 129; London Regional Art Gallery: pp. 53, 79, 123; Robert E. Mates, New York: p. 111; Metropolitan Museum, New York: p. 61; Montreal Museum of Fine Arts: pp. 19, 67, 76; The Museum of Modern Art, New York: pp. 25, 48; Courtesy National Gallery of Canada: pp. 11, 130; Larry Ostrom, Christie Lake Studios, Westport, Ontario: pp. 194, 195, 196, 197, 198, 199, 202, 203; Courtesy Harold Town: pp. 147, 183; Vancouver Art Gallery: p. 75; Michael J. Wilks, Windsor: pp. 10, 132. All other photos by Art Gallery of Ontario, Carlo Catanazzi.

Design: Ivan Holmes
Composition: Canadian Composition
Separations: Herzig Somerville Limited
Printing and Binding: D.W. Friesen & Sons Ltd.